Planning and the Private Sector

n C. Honey

The Experience in
Developing Countries

A Comparative Analysis

Planning and the Private Sector

The Dunellen Company, Inc., New York

International Standard Book Number 0–8424–0000–1.

Library of Congress Catalogue Card Number 71–119336.

Printed in the United States of America.

Designed by Anspach Grossman Portugal, Inc.

Preface

The role of the private sector in the development of national plans is a subject of considerable interest to modern economists and to those concerned with the politics of modernization. Clearly, the mustering of the experience of the private productive sectors—industrial, commercial, and agricultural—in assessing where a nation stands in its drive toward modernization and in laying down goals and programs for the future makes much sense. The broad rationale for such private participation in development planning has been analyzed by Dr. Theodore Geiger, Chief of International Studies of the National Planning Association (NPA), in his essay "Private Sector Participation in Development Planning" (National Planning Association, Center for Development Planning, April 1968), which explores the interactions of the cultural, social-institutional, attitudinal, and technical factors involved.

The empirical literature on planning is growing apace. Much of the important work has sought to fill the lacunae in our knowledge of what actually occurs in governmental planning processes around the world. One thinks, for example, of Albert Waterston's *Development Planning: Lessons of Experience* (Johns Hopkins Press, 1965) and a number of the publications emerging from Bertram Gross's National Planning Program at the Maxwell School, Syracuse University. These efforts have dealt in some part with the role of the private sector, but their goals have been broader and they have been prohibited by the scope of their endeavors from concentrating intensively on that particular aspect of the planning process.

The present two-part study devotes itself to the experience of the private sector in governmental planning in selected countries and to a consideration of ways in which the private sector is encouraged to perform in accordance with planned goals. It grows out of recent field visits to most of the countries whose experience is examined, and I hope that it will be of use and interest to government officials and to students of planning both in public service and in academic posts. When one is dealing with broad administrative and policy matters, immediate transferability of a colleague's experience to one's own area of responsibility is unlikely, but a good deal that is suggestive may be discovered in the record of others' work in the field.

Further, it is important that the "state of the art" be accurately understood, so that developing nations can muster the knowledge and resources to achieve modernization. Knowledge of theories and aspirations must be coupled with knowledge of where we now stand if there is to be effective forward motion. My coverage of individual national experience has been dictated by several considerations, such as the clear importance of the Indian and Malaysian experiments in planning; the desirability of looking at countries committed to stimulating private enterprise as well as at others traditionally skeptical of the private sector; geographic dispersion; and, of course, the practical limitations of resources.

This study was prepared in fulfillment of a subcontract from the NPA to the Institute of Public Administration, with which I was then affiliated. The assistance of Rodman P. Davis and Allan Austin in the preparation of materials for it has been very much appreciated.

Contents

Abbreviations

CDC	Commonwealth Development Corporation
CORFO	The Civilian Government's Development Corporation (Chile)
CSIO	Central Small Industries Organization (India)
EPU	Economic Planning Unit (Malaysia)
GNP	Gross National Product
IBRD	International Bank for Reconstruction and Development
ICICI	Industrial Credit and Investment Corporation of India
IDB	Industrial Development Bank (Pakistan)
IDBI	Industrial Bank of Israel
ILO	International Labour Organisation
IMDBI	Industrial and Mining Development Bank (Iran)
MDA	Mindanao Development Authority
MIDFL	Malayan Industrial Development Finance, Ltd.
NACIDA	National Cottage Industries Development Authority (Philippines)
NDPC	National Development Planning Committee (Malaysia)
NEC	National Economic Council (Philippines)
NPA	National Planning Association (U.S.)
ODEPLAN	Chilean Office of National Planning
PHILCUSA	Philippine Commission for United States Aid
PIA	Program Implementation Agency (Philippines)
PICIC	Pakistan Industrial Credit and Investment Corporation
PIFC	Pakistan Industrial Finance Corporation
SPO	State Planning Organization (Turkey)

Planning and the Private Sector

Part 1 The Organization and Process of Private Participation in Development Planning

1 Consultative Arrangements in the French Model

The models, ideas and approaches which underlie systems of planning in the developing nations have, of course, an array of sources. These are to be found in the literature on planning; in the experiences of plan-oriented industrialized nations, such as France and the Soviet Union; in the ideas of advisors assisting governments with their planning aspirations; and in the formulations of theoreticians like the English Fabian socialists.

The French Planning System

Both because of its apparent success and because it is the product of a politically open society, the French planning system has had widespread appeal as a model to be followed, to a greater or lesser degree, by developing countries.[1] Begun after World War II, French planning is now in its fifth plan period, 1966-70. While it is legitimate to describe it as a well-established system, it in fact involved a good deal of experimentation and modification when experience indicated the need to change assumptions and procedures.

French planning has two stages: the first normative or goal-setting in broad terms; the second designed to convert the goals into more or less specific targets. In the first stage the desired growth rate is set, usually at about 5 percent of GNP per year. Targets are then determined for overall consumption and also for sectors or areas (*e.g.*, industry, agriculture, the various geographic regions of France, etc.). In the course of arriving at these policy guidelines, the government encourages discussion, debate, and the presentation of alternative views from virtually all interested sectors of society. It does this by proposing policy alternatives for the consideration of employers, farmers, labor, and other groups who are represented in the Economic and Social Council, a consultative body to the government. The Council's views, after considerable debate, are made public together with those of the government, and in practice they serve to modify the government's plan.

The task of converting broad goals into fairly specific targets is in part that of the official planning agency, the Commissariat du Plan. But much of the detailed work is farmed out to specialized bodies or planning commissions having both public and private representatives. Since they are the sources of data and practical experience, their involvement is likely to assure cooperation in the plan's implementation.

Hackett points out,

> There were twenty-seven commissions for the Fourth Plan, divided into two sorts, 'vertical' and 'horizontal.' Altogether, with the working parties that each can set up with members co-opted from outside the commissions, over 3,000 people were associated with drafting the Fourth Plan, and about the same number. . . in preparing the Fifth. Membership of the commissions comprises civil servants (all the main ministries being represented), representatives of the nationalized industries, private employers, farmers and trade unionists. The vertical commissions are concerned with particular branches of economic activity (energy, steel, chemicals, agriculture, and so on). The horizontal commissions deal with general aspects such as overall balance, manpower and regional development.[2]

A number of functions are performed by the commissions, including providing statistical data to the Commissariat du Plan; assessing developments in their sector in relationship to projected GNP; reporting on major policy issues relevant to the goals being set, *e.g.*, availability of trained manpower, investment requirements, pricing policies; and recommending changes in such matters as tax policies and manpower development schemes. The commissions not only provide government with relevant factual and judgmental information; they are being informed in the process, and thus become a source of leadership for plan implementation. This is particularly important, since the final version of the plan sets targets not for individual firms but, rather, for branches of industry. Thus, cooperation rather than dependence on detailed control is an absolute essential for success in plan fulfillment.

Those who are impressed with the accomplishments of French planning (and indeed the record of plan fulfillment is noteworthy) do not always take account of the unique characteristics which underlie the system. Albert Waterston has pointed out certain of them, not to detract in any way from the significance of French planning but, rather, to provide perspective for those who seek to emulate it. The French approach is

> based on cartelized industries, much of it nationalized, public investments which approximate half of total investment in the country, along with a nationalized credit system and government controls over private industrial financing, a weak trade union movement and a tradition of close cooperation between business and government. In addition, it relies on a civil service system of especial competence.[3]

Among those developing nations that have been influenced by French consultative approaches to planning are Morocco, Tunisia, Tanzania, and Chile.

Morocco

In Morocco the Superior Planning Council was established by law in 1957. It was made up of 24 members, including most of the Cabinet, representatives of the National Consultative Assembly, three agricultural representatives, three union representatives, and one each from handicrafts, industry, and commerce. The nongovernmental representatives were chosen by the agricultural, labor, and business associations. The Council was to be assisted by a finance committee and a number of specialized commissions. As Douglas Ashford points out, "The planning organization was almost identical to the French organization."[4] But although the machinery was extensive, the government made little use of it in the early years. An interim report, consisting primarily of the uncoordinated plans of the various ministries, was produced for the years 1958-59, but the Superior Planning Council did not meet during this period. Late in 1959 the Council was called into session, together with its 15 specialized commissions. It was intended that the commissions work on the development of the projected 1960-64 five-year plan, but their labors revealed that they were more under the influence of the dominant interests in the commissions than concerned with the broad needs of the economy.

In 1960 the Superior Planning Council met to consider a five-year plan. The members were, however, widely in disagreement, and the plan itself seemed to lack central purpose and concept. In spite of deep disagreements about the plan, it was approved by the King and became law. Ashford notes that the bitterness of internal politics had a marked impact on the plan:

> No influential figure or group could afford to ignore the national planning effort, but neither could such figures or groups agree. By the time the country had prepared a plan. . .political forces had diverged so greatly that it was almost impossible to give the plan any meaning in the internal political life of the country. . . .The monarchy failed to rally support for the plan, while discouraging more articulate political groups by arbitrarily imposing favored projects and denying basic powers to the planning agency.[5]

Thus, despite machinery which, if used, would have encouraged widespread participation in plan formulation, the nature of the prevailing political leadership was such as to preclude this.

Tunisia

The Tunisian situation appears in rather sharp contrast to the developments in Morocco. Deeply influenced by three generations of French occupation, Tunisians have an understanding of the role of bureaucracy and an appreciation of the significance of planning as an aid to the development of their country. Their single-party system, under the strong leadership of President Bourguiba, has provided a sense of unity and purpose. In the late 1950's, however, when planning became an important issue, there was considerable opposition to the President from the labor movement. Among other things, he was charged with improvisation and a failure to deal with economic and social issues on a long-term basis. In early 1958, in part as response to such criticisms, the National Planning Council was established, with responsibility for setting economic goals and priorities, for proposing sectoral development programs, and for recommending the means of financing development as well as stimulating the private sector. The Council included key figures from the President's office, the ministers concerned with social and economic affairs, two representatives from the National Assembly, and four from national organizations—labor, commerce, agriculture, and banking.

During the succeeding three years, the Council did relatively little, but the President, in this period, was consolidating his own political position and informing the public about the economic issues which the nation must address. In 1961, a new superministry was created, headed by the Secretary of State for Planning and Finance, and with strong Presidential backing, work was begun on the preparation of the national plan. The first document was essentially the perspectives or forecasts on which detailed planning would be based. It was completed in six months and was prepared largely by technicians assembled from the various ministries of the government. There followed two months of widespread discussion on the broad perspectives of the plan. A detailed plan for 1962-64 was proposed late in 1961. Meanwhile, early in 1961, the Economic and Social Council, which had been authorized by the constitution, was assembled, and about a year later it received and studied the detailed plan. Composed of four subcommissions—dealing with industry, agriculture, transport, and organization—and broadly representative of public and private interests, the Economic and Social Council offered a vehicle for the expression of views on the plan from the several sectors of the community. Subsequently, a political party organ, the Neo-Destour's National Council, which included many merchants and businessmen, reviewed and approved the plan. It then was returned to the government and before adoption was examined by five subcommissions of the National Assembly, dealing with industry and commerce, social affairs, agriculture, finance, and manpower requirements.

The Tunisian approach to plan formulation, involving extensive consultation with the institutional forces of the country, is akin to that used by the French. But President Bourguiba, in the presence of political factors unique to Tunisia, preceded the inauguration of planning consultation with a campaign that both consolidated his position and served to educate the public. Certainly, a conclusion to be drawn from the Tunisian experience is that the coupling of the machinery of consultation with strong political leadership is imperative to success in plan formulation.

Tanzania

In Tanzania, as Professor Fred G. Burke has observed, "there is within government considerable admiration for the French approach to national planning. This, when added to the appointment of a French director of planning, may be indicative of the direction that future organization and activities will take."[6] That French approaches to planning can be useful for Tanzania without major adaptation is difficult to imagine. A large, sparsely populated, relatively poorly endowed agricultural nation, it has several characteristics that set it far apart from centralized, industrialized, cosmopolitan France. Tanzania's African population consists of approximately 125 distinct tribal groupings, which vary greatly in size. Its governmental heritage is colonial British. It is a primary-product producer, almost totally dependent for foreign exchange on the sale of sisal and a few other agricultural goods abroad. It imports nearly all of the manufactured goods it consumes. Thus, its economy is dependent on foreign markets and price levels, and its capacity to control its economic development is seriously circumscribed.

The government established in 1962 the Economic Development Commission, which included a ministerial committee, a coordinating committee, and a planning secretariat. The coordinating committee is made up of the permanent secretaries of the several participating ministries, and the planning secretariat has sections concerned with plan preparation and plan implementation. In 1964, following the union with Zanzibar, there was created the Directorate of Development Planning, which became the technical advisor on development. But the EDC continued to be the policy arm of the government on planning and development. In July 1964, the *Tanganyika Five-Year Plan for Economic and Social Development, 1st July 1964–30th June 1969*, was issued. It was prepared by the planning secretariat, working cooperatively with the ministries. This plan was prepared during a one-year period in which there were three phases of activity. These were described in a statement by the Minister of State, A. Z. N. Swai, as follows:

> The first phase consisted in determining and analysing long-term social and economic objectives for 1980. This involved the examination of past rates of growth in the economy and the diagnosis of the main obstacles

to progress which had been encountered and the prescription of structural changes to overcome them. Higher rates of growth were then tested against the human, material and financial resources likely to be available and against the conditions likely to be encountered in world markets. This process led to the submission of a report in August 1963, to the Economic Development Commission on the policies to be adopted in the social and economic fields for the achievement of these long-term objectives.

The second phase consisted in determining the intermediate stages likely to be achieved by 1970 in progress towards 1980 targets and their significance in terms of the production of the various sectors. Sectoral production was tested against expected demand both in domestic and external markets. In the Agricultural Sector the projected capacity of production was compared with estimates supplied by the Ministry of Agriculture and Regional Development Committees of likely output in 1970. In the Industrial Sector various assumptions were made concerning the adaptation of the existing East Africa Common Market to promote a better distribution of industrial activity within the area. In the other sectors of Transport, Commerce, Construction, Public Utilities and Miscellaneous Services the level of activity was related to the probable needs of the two preceding sectors. The financial and manpower resources for achieving the target level of activity by 1970 were computed, leading to the formulation of policies on the one hand for involving the cooperation of the private sector and on the other for seeking assistance abroad. . . .

The second phase led to the submission. . .to the EDC of a Draft Outline Five-Year Plan showing the volume of investment necessary in the various sectors of the economy and the action needed to achieve the targets set for 1970.

Finally, the third stage consisted in the drawing up as far as possible of specific and coordinated development programmes within the framework of the Outline Plan and in finalizing the present document. The production of the Five-Year Plan is the result of close collaboration and cooperation between the various Government Ministries, Regional Development Committees, the Chambers of Commerce, and the National Union of Tanganyika Workers. This cooperation which gave rise to the convening of over 60 working parties and meetings is ample evidence that the document has been a truly joint national effort.[7]

Since independence, Julius Nyerere, the President of Tanzania, has been engaged in creating a nation out of a country whose populace is primarily tribal in loyalties and which has little historical sense of nationhood. Reference to the French experience has encouraged wide consultation; and although most of the institutional factors which motivated the French planning system are lacking in Tanzania, the philosophy of participation has had its own utility as a contributor to the nation-building process. This is of no small significance, particularly for those modernizing countries whose national identity is more a product of colonial determinations than of deep-seated ethnic, historical, or geographic imperatives.

Chile

That Chilean planning might be influenced by French consultative experience is not surprising. For more than 20 years, industry, agriculture, and other organized private associations have participated as voting members on executive boards of the major quasi-governmental regulatory and investment agencies. Of particular interest in the Chilean situation is the way in which participation in the planning process has been modified to encourage the viewpoints of more liberal elements, representative of and sympathetic to the objectives of the Christian Democratic government.

The Chilean Office of National Planning (ODEPLAN) is the technical secretariat of the Economic Committee, which determines broad policy issues. The committee includes the Minister of Finance, who serves as Chairman; the Ministers of Economics, Labor, and Agriculture; the Director of the Bureau of the Budget; the head of the National Bank; and the President of the government's development corporation, CORFO.

Each ministry has a planning office, which is responsible to the Minister but receives technical guidance from ODEPLAN. Sectoral planning is carried on in these units. For purposes of regional planning, Chile's 25 provinces have been grouped into 10 regions, plus Santiago. Regional councils have the task of preparing regional development plans within guidelines set by ODEPLAN.

In the process of plan preparation, sectoral, regional, and national, extensive consultation and participation is required. But the present reform government does not find the old forms of participation, which involved actual sharing in decision-making on the part of private-sector representatives, to be particularly satisfactory.

At present, a new framework of participation is being created, emphasizing involvement of the community rather than the private sector. Each sector will have its own institutional arrangement, built around the idea of rational, intellectual involvement. The goal will be to exchange information and to find consensus on sectoral and project plans. Whether the old associations and organizations, which so frequently represented vested interests, can be persuaded to extend their memberships, democratize their voting rules, and in other ways open themselves to new and more dynamic influences, remains to be seen. Otherwise, government may take the initiative in setting up industrial, labor, regional and project-oriented advisory groups, in the manner of the French planners.

The Chilean experience highlights a significant aspect of the participatory approach to planning. Participants may reflect, within the orbit of their expertise or competence, views that are dynamic, progressive, and socially responsive. However, they may also express narrow, limited opinions, reflective of an entrenched *ancien régime* Or, presumably, they may simply provide technical responses to planning ideas, proposals, and policies. However, the latter is not usually the limit of the contribution sought by governments in inviting private-sector participation.

On the government's side, its stance with respect to modernization will determine how it responds to the advice it receives. In general, modernizing governments are inclined to reduce the independent influence of the economic and social establishment and to favor strong government action. To accept indiscriminately participants from the private sector by no means assures that the government will receive advice of which it can make use. Nor does it assure that all significant viewpoints in the private sector will be heard. Thus, careful attention to the agents of participation is an essential of the planning process.

Notes

1. For detailed consideration of French planning, see Pierre Bauchet, *Economic Planning: The French Experience* (New York: Praeger, 1964); John Hackett and Anne-Marie Hackett, *Economic Planning in France* (Cambridge, Mass.: Harvard University Press, 1963).

2. John Hackett, *Economic Planning in France: Its Relation to the Policies of the Developed Countries of Western Europe* (New York: Asia Publishing House, for the Council for Economic Education, 1965), p. 24.

3. Albert Waterston, *Development Planning: Lessons of Experience* (Baltimore: Johns Hopkins Press, 1965), p. 380.

4. Douglas Elliott Ashford, *Morocco-Tunisia: Politics and Planning* (Syracuse, N.Y.: Syracuse University Press, 1965), p. 13.

5. *Ibid.*, p. 17.

6. Fred G. Burke, *Taganyika: Preplanning* (Syracuse, N.Y.: Syracuse University Press, 1965), pp. 56-57.

7. The United Republic of Tanganyika and Zanzibar, *Tanganyika Five-Year Plan for Economic and Social Development, 1st July 1964–30th June 1969*, Vol. I, "General Analysis" (Dar es Salaam: The Government Printer, 1964), pp. 2-3.

2 Detailed Central Planning

Although India is the leading example of a developing country whose central government has attempted to carry on detailed economic planning embracing both the public and the private sectors and there is a tendency to assume that Indian planning practice is typical of that followed by most developing countries, the contrary is actually the case. Turkey, however, underwent a social revolution under Ataturk that left a heritage with respect to the role of government and the attitude toward the private sector which is, to a degree, similar to that found among Indian planners. A comparison of the detailed central planning of these two countries, therefore, is of value in the context of this study.

India

Among the modernizing nations committed to government by popularly chosen leaders, India is the largest in terms of size and population. It also has the most profound and complex socioeconomic problems, and its success in dealing with these problems is widely viewed as a test of democracy. India's program for modernization through planning is more clear-cut and fully institutionalized than that of any other developing country. Its leadership sees India as a democratic socialist state for which the concepts of the English Fabians have provided the basic intellectual rationale.

At independence the leaders of India faced the task of modernizing a near-classic example of a colonial economy. The nation provided raw materials, largely cotton and jute, for the industries of advanced nations and, in return, imported manufactured goods. Eighty percent of the population lived in primitive villages; 85 percent were illiterate; and a population explosion was under way, largely because the high birth rate had not adjusted itself to the lower mortality rates produced by British public health measures. Under circumstances such as these, the issue was not whether India would plan, but how she would do it.

Although the Constitution of 1950 contains no specifications for economic-planning machinery, its provisions for basic economic policy imply that the government will play a strong role in the economy. The leaders of independence were well aware of the necessity for economic planning, and the parliamentary form of government was selected for the new nation partly because it was believed that it would be more likely to assure the cooperation between executive and legislature necessary for the facilitation of economic development. The principal planning bodies, the Planning Commission and the National Development Council, were established by Cabinet resolution, the former in 1950 and the latter in 1952.

The Planning Commission is a staff agency designed to prepare national plans for economic development. Four of the nine members of the Commission are ministers of the central government, whose participation, it was hoped, might insure that planning would not be isolated from line activity. There is some reason to believe that this policy partially backfired during the early years of economic planning, since the ministers' interest in sectoral planning tended to hamper development of the concept of integrated planning.

Dissatisfaction among the states because of lack of state representation on the Planning Commission led to the formation of the National Development Council. The Council, composed of the Prime Minister of India, the chief ministers of states, and members of the Planning Commission, is a reviewing body designed to assist the progress of the Planning Commission and to approve its plans.

Preparation of Five-Year Plans

The process of preparing a five-year plan in India is elaborate.[1] Initial analyses of the state of the economy and a review of production trends, rates of economic growth, etc., are undertaken about three years in advance of the start of a plan period.

Preliminary judgments about the state of the economy are submitted by the Planning Commission to the Cabinet and also to the National Development Council, and the rate of growth to be assumed for the plan period is tentatively set, together with identification of objectives and problems which should receive special attention.

Next, the Planning Commission sets up a series of working groups composed of its own specialists and others drawn from the various ministries. State governments are advised to constitute similar working groups, whose efforts can be coordinated with those of the national groups. These deal with such subjects as financial resources, agriculture, irrigation, power, steel, fuel, education, scientific research, health and family planning, housing. The working group on financial reserves concerns itself with an estimation of external and internal resources in both the private and the public sector. Its membership includes officials from the Planning Commission, the Ministry of Finance, and the Reserve Bank of India.

At the same time that the working groups are preparing their reports the Planning Commission constitutes panels of experts, drawn largely from outside the government, to advise on broad aspects of policy in such fields as science, economics, land reform, and education.

As a result of these efforts, a draft memorandum is prepared which highlights major policy issues for Cabinet consideration. Subsequently, a draft outline of the plan is developed in the Planning Commission. This is published and widely circulated for comment, going to central government ministries, state governments, and District Development Councils. Nongovernmental bodies are also given an opportunity to review this draft. It is examined in both houses of Parliament and in a number of parliamentary committees. Simultaneously, state plans are reviewed in detail by the Planning Commission. Finally, a new memorandum on the plan is prepared for consideration. This leads to the final report on the plan which, again after extensive review, is published and presented to Parliament for general approval.

Role of the Private Sector

During the early years of independence, the government of India was inclined to feel that nationalization was a universal cure-all for industry. A Parliamentary declaration in December 1945 stated that economic policy should point to the achievement of the "socialist pattern of society." However, the socialist pattern of society in India is far from the conventional one. In 1958 nearly 90 percent of the country's enterprises, generating approximately 92 percent of the national income, were in private hands. The respective roles of the public and private sectors of Indian industry were outlined in the statement on industrial development policy read in Parliament on April 30, 1956. Industry is classified in three categories:

a. Category I—17 industries the development of which is the exclusive State monopoly. Included are defense industry; atomic energy; iron and steel; coal; mineral oils; mining of iron ore, gold, diamonds, etc.; aircraft; air and railway transport, shipbuilding, and the generation of electricity.

b. Category II—12 industries in which the state will generally take the initiative in starting new enterprises but may transfer them eventually to private owners. In this category "private enterprise will also be expected to supplement the effort of the state whether on its own or with state participation." Included are aluminum, machine tools, antibiotics and other essential drugs, fertilizers, certain minerals, basic and intermediate products required by chemical industries, sea transport, road transport, ferro-alloys and tool steel, synthetic rubber, chemical pulp, and carbonization of coal.

c. Category III—all fields not otherwise specified, left to the initiative and enterprise of the private sector.[2]

While the facts belie the notion that India is a socialist state in terms of public ownership of the vast percentage of production facilities, the government's pronouncements on this subject have not, until quite recently, been particularly reassuring to the private sector. Many of the government's leaders were educated in Great Britain during the era when Fabian socialism had a wide intellectual following. They have tended to speak in ideological terms, implying criticism of both the economic and moral validity of private enterprise.

For its part, Indian private enterprise has suffered from excessive domination by family interests and from caste consciousness. But it has grudgingly accepted the need for planning and is beginning to recognize that its management capacities must be broadened, both through university training and expansion of the base of its leadership.

The role of the private sector in planning has been somewhat ambiguous. The initial and secondary stages of plan development, as previously noted, are carried out by the Planning Commission and the National Development Council, neither of which has representatives from the private sector. During the second, or study and analysis, stage the Planning Commission sets up working groups. For the first three plans these were composed only of government officials. However, for the Fourth Five-Year Plan the working groups included representatives from private industry and labor as well as professional consultants.

At the time the draft memorandum is submitted to the Cabinet for discussion, not much is known concerning the scope of plans of the private sector, even the corporate private sector, and the memorandum can do no more than outline the larger magnitudes involved. During the nationwide consideration of the draft, there is consultation between the private sector and state and district development councils, but this primarily involves small industries.

The official Indian attitude toward the role of the private sector in planning may perhaps be summarized as having moved from a view that the planning function is essentially a government task to a recognition that it is useful to draw upon the knowledge and data available in the private sector for plan preparation. The step beyond this, namely, enlisting the positive involvement of the private sector in the setting of broad national goals and objectives from the earliest stages of the planning process, apparently has not arrived yet. This view is confirmed by A.H. Hanson who, at the conclusion of his exhaustive study of Indian planning, commented:

Procedurally. . .the work of the (Planning) Commission would seem to be nearly as satisfactory as one could reasonably expect, given the socio-political setting. There are two criticisms, however, which ought to be made. The first concerns the relationship between the Planning Commission and the private sector. Although this has immensely improved of recent years, it is still not good enough. Perhaps more devoted to the socialist pattern of society than the majority of their countrymen, the officials of the Commission, while recognizing in theory the important role that the private businessman has to play, are in practice inclined to treat him with suspicion and hold him at arm's length. . . . Consultation with private business is, as we have seen, both frequent and organized; but, as far as the Commission is concerned, it is perhaps regarded as slightly peripheral activity. Too much of it, one might argue, is left to the Ministry of Commerce and Industry, which has tended to become a business ministry, ideologically oriented towards its clients, and inclined to regard itself as the private sector rival of the public sector Commission. There is now a strong case for a more direct association of private business with the planning process, through devices comparable with the French *Commissions de Modernisation.*[3]

The Indian government's planning experience vis-à-vis the private sector suggests a progression from dogma toward practicality. It indicates the importance of continuing reappraisal of the doctrinal bases of relationships with the private sector, since ideology can stultify as well as inspire. This is especially necessary in the developing nations, for they are continually pressed to find ready solutions and are inevitably limited in the time and resources available for pragmatic experimentation.

Turkey

In Turkey in the early 1920's, under the leadership of Ataturk, traditionalism of all kinds came under scrutiny and reevaluation, and the dominant role of the citizenry was proclaimed. Ataturk's program of populism emphasized the placing of power, authority, sovereignty, and administration in the hands of the people.

In the late 1920's, Ataturk and his followers had observed, on the one hand, the chaotic consequences of capitalism inadequately regulated and, on the other, what appeared to them to be the initial success of the Soviet experiment. Without adopting a doctrinaire position, Ataturk undertook a variety of reforms which he hoped would result in economic and social modernization and which he described as Turkish statism.

Inducements were offered to industry, in the form of tax advantages, to establish new plants. The five-year plan launched in the early 1930's placed under government management or supervision a wide variety of industrial plants. Two important banks were established in this period; the Sumer Bank, to promote industry; and the Eti Bank, to operate state-owned or nationalized mines. Government monopolies controlled a number of important products.

The death of Ataturk in 1938, the advent of World War II, the rise of Soviet imperialism, and the coming to power of the Menderes government, all had severe repercussions on the process of modernization launched by Ataturk. Following the revolution of 1960, a new constitution was adopted that affirmed the important role of the state in economic planning and development:

> Economic and social life shall be regulated in a manner consistent with justice, and the principle of full employment, with the objective of assuring for everyone a standard of living befitting human dignity.
>
> It is the duty of the State to encourage economic, social and cultural development by democratic processes and for this purpose to enhance national savings, to give priority to those investments which promote public welfare, and to draw up development projects.[4]
>
> ...Development Projects and the State Planning Organization: Economic, social and cultural development is based on a plan. Development is carried out according to this plan.[5]

In 1960, Law No. 91 was passed, creating the State Planning Organization (SPO) under the Prime Minister. Administrative control over the SPO is exercised by the Deputy Prime Minister. In summary, its functions are to prepare long-range and short-term plans and to assist in implementing and evaluating them. It is also required to "propose measures which will encourage and regulate the activities of the private sector to perform in harmony with the plan's objectives."[6]

Plans of the SPO are reviewed by the High Planning Council for their adequacy and relevance to the goals which have been set by the Council of Ministers. The High Planning Council, which is a subcommittee of the Council of Ministers and acts for it in matters dealing with the plan, is composed of the Prime Minister (or the Deputy Prime Minister), three ministers elected by the Council of Ministers, the Undersecretary for Planning, and the heads of the Economic Planning Department, the Social Planning Department and the Coordinating Department of the SPO.

The operating head of the SPO is the Undersecretary for Planning, who reports to the Deputy Prime Minister. Within the SPO, the Economic Planning Department has units which develop long-term plans, annual programs, and financial and sector programs. It conducts studies needed for long- and short-term plans and deals with general and regional problems. The Social Planning Department has a research and a planning section. The Coordination Department, with financial, legal, research, and other functions, recommends financial and legal measures to implement plans within both the public and the private sector.

Turkey's First Five-Year Plan

Turkey's initial five-year plan (1963-67) was prepared in consultation with Professor Jan Tinbergen, the Dutch economist and planner. Decisions about the general nature of the plan were made with the aid of an advisory board composed of representatives from the fields of science, administration, politics, trade, and industry.

The plan, as drawn up, contained a broad program of development for 15 years and five-year sectoral programs covering agriculture, mining, manufacturing, construction, power, transportation, communications and services. The plan also considered manpower problems, regional planning and development, and implementation policy.

Since detailed regional studies were, for the most part, not completed by the time of the plan's issuance, it was anticipated that the annual programs would give more attention to regional development. The emphasis in the regional analyses was to be on areas of potential development, on backward regions, and on metropolitan areas.

The Turkish Plan of 1963-67 is exceptional for a variety of reasons. Turkey had had a long-standing interest in and periodic experience with planning. The plan provided for a well-developed administrative structure. It was designed with the assistance of sophisticated planning economists, such as Professor Tinbergen, and was to be instituted within an affirmative constitutional and legal framework and implemented in a country where the prevailing attitude among politicians, professionals, and populace was planning. In the translation of the plan into annual programs, there has been a good deal of specificity about sectors, subsectors, and budget requirements.

For all the competence of the Turkish Plan, however, certain persistent problems have inhibited its execution. Ministerial autonomy vis-à-vis the Prime Minister and problems of ministerial control have made coordination difficult. The SPO, in the eyes of some observers, lacks sufficient power and prestige to meet its responsibilities: for example, it has not played a major role with respect to coordinating external aid. It has not been easy to find and retain competent planning personnel. Government salaries, including those in state enterprises, compare unfavorably with salaries in private industry. Private investors, while they have exceeded the amount of investment planned, tend not to put their funds into priority areas identified in the plan.

The 1963-67 development plan discusses the nature of the mixed economy in Turkey and the rules which govern its operation as follows:

> The private sector alone cannot realize all the conditions necessary for economic development. Economic development will be attained by accelerating investment and making basic changes in the structure and methods of production. These changes cannot be accomplished solely by entrepreneurs who adjust their activities according to market conditions. The change from an underdeveloped and stagnant economy to a progressive and dynamic one may be achieved through systematic and rational measures taken by the central authority. The development of Turkey's primitive economic structure into a more advanced production system was made possible by public investments and the activities of the State Economic Enterprises.[7]

The plan also discusses the problem of capital formation, noting that to maintain a growth rate of 7 percent, most of the increase in national income must be channeled into investments. Private-sector savings are to be encouraged by tax and credit polciies. Also, the public funds derived from taxes and state enterprises will be devoted primarily to economic development.

Public-sector investments are to be for the purposes of (a) creating infrastructure, including power supply, irrigation and dams, transportation, and traditional public services, such as education, health, and communications; (b) increasing the productivity and efficiency of state economic enterprises; eliminating bottlenecks where private enterprise has not moved in; mobilizing private and foreign capital in mixed enterprises; and creating or continuing state monopolies or controling injurious private monopolies.

On the subject of relationships between the public and private sectors, the plan says that the same rules of economic policy will apply to both. The state will make known its fiscal, monetary, price, and foreign trade and investment policies, for the guidance of the private sector. It also will issue information on economic developments in general and on the various sectors, through publication of quarterly economic reports. State enterprises will follow a price policy designed to yield maximum profits, and ordinarily prices will not be set below cost. Interest rates and terms and incentives for the repayment of interest and capital will be determined by sectors and be kept in line with plan targets. Protective tariffs will be applied selectively and in a nondiscriminatory manner to both public and private enterprises.

In the drafting of the plan, the role of the private sector was limited to participation, by a few private economists, on an advisory board which considered broad objectives and strategy and to service on various of the sectoral committees. The actual extent of participation varied greatly among these committees.

Attitude of the Private Sector

The principal spokesman for the private sector is the Union of Chambers of Commerce, Industry, and Commodity Exchanges. The Union represents 100 chambers of commerce, 3 chambers of industry, and 37 commodity exchanges. Its membership also includes industrial establishments in the public sector. In the absence of an active tradition of voluntary organizations, the Union was created in 1950 by the government (Law No. 5590) in part for the purpose of advising it on economic conditions affecting business and industry. The Union is also responsible for arbitrating professional disputes between its members and for reporting on the economic situation in Turkey. A general assembly of the Union members meets annually to elect the

Board of Directors, which in turn appoints the Secretary-General.

This organization is a major source of information to the government on industry's views with respect to public policy. It prepared a critique of the five-year plan in which questions were raised about the division of responsibility for new investment between government and private industry. But the attitude of the Union toward the five-year plan is not unfavorable. Members of the Union are encouraged to invest in areas which the plan has identified as important to development. And the Union has proposed to the government certain measures to stimulate investment in line with the plan, such as the selective use of customs duties, encouragement of private savings, and capital formation through investment in securities and the formation of stock companies.

The Union is not represented on the High Planning Council. It does sit on the Advisory Board, but the Board meets only once a year, and the Union believes it should participate in the work of the Council also. Certainly if this opportunity were provided, the views of industry representatives could be brought to bear on the whole planning process, a desirable development in the eyes of the Council, where although there are strong bureaucratic and traditional favors in favor of statism, there is also commitment to a mixed economy.

Notes

1. India National Planning Commission, *The Planning Process* (New Delhi: October, 1963).

2. Adapted from Indian Investment Center, *Investing in India. . .Basic Facts of the Indian Economy* (New Delhi, 1962), pp. 76-77.

3. A.H. Hanson, *The Process of Planning: A Study of India's Five-Year Plans, 1950-64* (New York: Oxford University Press, 1966), p. 532.

4. Turkey, *Constitution of July 1961*, Art. 41: "The Regulation of Economic and Social Life."

5. *Ibid.*, Art. 129: "Development."

6. Turkey, Law No. 91 (Sept. 30, 1960): "Concerning the Establishment of the State Planning Organization."

7. Turkey, *First Five-Year Development Plan, 1963-1967* (Ankara: State Planning Organization, 1963), p. 55.

3

Macro Planning with Private-Sector Encouragement

A number of modernizing nations are basically private-enterprise oriented. Illustrative are Malaysia, Pakistan, Iran, and the Philippines. All of these countries are at the same time pursuing vigorous programs of development under government leadership and are having recourse, in varying degrees, to formal planning.

Malaysia

In Malaysia two circumstances are of particular significance in shaping public-private relationships. First is the fact that, because it was a part of Britain's former colonial empire, the country has a strong tradition of respect for the ideal of self-government, of law, of responsibility and integrity in the civil service, and of an economy primarily ordered to private entrepreneurship.

Second is the supremacy of rubber in the economy. The prosperity of the states of Malaysia is, of course, attributable to that commodity. Rubber production continues to expand, encouraged by government policy, in spite of the decline of rubber prices in recent years. While it is recognized that the economy of Malaysia is overly dependent on rubber and that the development of cheap synthetics can have severe economic repercussions, rubber still is the dominant economic element of the country.

At the founding of Malaysia, in September 1963, each member state had its own development scheme. Malaya's Second Five-Year Plan covered the years 1961-65; Sabah's Six-Year Plan was for 1959-64; Singapore's Four-Year Plan covered the period 1961-64; and Sarawak was completing its Four-Year Plan for 1959-63. It had been estimated that not until 1966 would the states merge their development plans, but with the separation of Singapore from the federation, the Malayan Plan, which was the most highly developed, assumed a central position in federation planning.

The broad objective of Malaya's Second Five-Year Plan was to provide opportunities for the rural population to improve their economic and social well-being; to assure employment of the country's working-age population; to raise per capita output and protect per capita living standards against the adverse effects of a possible decline in rubber prices; to expand production, particularly in agriculture; to encourage industrial expansion; and to improve and expand social services, housing and utilities for both rural and urban populations.

The First Five-Year Plan had been essentially a collection of projects, largely uncoordinated and unrationalized. The Second Five-Year Plan set broad guidelines for the economy. It envisaged that during the plan period the total development outlay would be $5,050 million, of which $2,150 million would be public investment and $2,900 million private. Subsequently, the annual plans incorporated in the budget estimates have raised the levels of public investment, and public investment now equals private.

The initiative for industrial development was left to private enterprise under the plan. Public investment was allocated among programs in agriculture, transport and communications, public utilities, and social services. Information on individual projects was not provided, and priorities were not assigned.

The structure of Malayan planning has aroused considerable interest because of the degree to which there has been decentralized participation in plan preparation and because of the informational and control features of plan execution. A permanent body, called the National Development Planning Committee (NDPC), composed of leading civil servants, is appointed by the government. Annual capital budgets are reviewed by the NDPC for submission to the Cabinet and Parliament. The NDPC also advises the government on the progress of the development programs. The secretariat of the NDPC, the Economic Planning Unit (EPU), located in the Prime

Minister's Department, is staffed with local as well as foreign economists.

The ministries and departments have been encouraged to establish departmental planning and research units, and a limited number have done so. Several more have designated planning officials. The EPU maintains liaison with these offices and individuals, seeking to bring into the central planning effort as much guidance and direction as possible from the ministries.

Formulation and Execution of the Plan

The manner in which much of the content of the five-year plan is formulated in the districts of Malaya has been described as follows:

> Each of the states that composed the former Federation of Malaya, save one, is divided into several administrative districts, seventy of them in all. The chief administrator of each district is a civil servant known as the District Officer. In each district there is a Rural Development Committee, under the chairmanship of the District Officer, which includes in its membership representatives of various state and federal ministries. One of the duties of the District Officer is to organize a Village Development Committee in each of the kampongs in his district. Nearly a third of the kampongs now have such committees.
>
> The District Officer and other members of the District Development Committee visit the towns and kampongs in the district and determine, through discussions with town boards or councils, kampong development committees, or kampong headmen, the nature of the improvements that the people want. These may include roads and bridges, water supplies, electric plants, telephone stations, small river-clearance and irrigation projects, processing and marketing facilities for local products, new small industries, health centers, school buildings, and playing fields. Such projects give expression to conscious local needs. To them the District Development Committee may add projects of its own, such as those involving the clearance of land for settlement. All these, when brought together by the District Officer, constitute the development proposals for the district.[1]

The district plan is then summarized graphically in a single volume, which includes maps and charts to give a visual presentation of the district's development scheme. Characteristically, the plan is located in the District Operation's Room, which is the headquarters of the Rural Development Committee.

Officials of state and federal ministries operating in the districts forward to their respective ministries relevant district proposals. They also present district proposals to the State Development Committees. These latter bodies review the proposals from the districts in their states, make modifications and additions, such as state-wide irrigation, drainage, or hydroelectric projects, and forward their recommendations to the appropriate federal ministries and departments.

At the same time, the municipalities within each state, which are governed by elected councils, forward their development proposals that are to be financed with federal, rather than municipal, funds to the relevant federal ministries.

At the time the Second Five-Year Plan was prepared, the planning units or planning offices in the federal ministries and departments reviewed and evaluated the proposals emanating from districts, states, and municipalities. They approved some, rejected others, and added projects of their own in such fields as transport, communications, and the promotion of industrial development. The results were then transmitted to the Treasury and the Economic Planning Unit for preparation of the total plan.

The process of translating the plan into annual budgets is carried out through a system of consultation and hearings. Ultimate responsibility for the budget rests with the Cabinet, which is aided in adapting the plan to annual fiscal realities by the NDPC and its secretariat, the EPU. The NDPC's recommendations, after approval by the Cabinet, become the development estimates for the coming year. These are submitted to Parliament, debated and acted upon. Parliament's authorizations then permit allocations of funds to the ministries, states, districts, and municipalities.

As the development projects are executed, there is continuous evaluation, observation, and reporting on the part of responsible officials. District personnel are required to report progress to the State Development Committees, as well as to appropriate state and federal ministries. They must also keep the EPU informed. Extensive direct observation is carried on by members of district and state development committees, as well as by representatives of the federal ministries and even by the Deputy Prime Minister. A national operating room is maintained in the capital, where it is

possible to examine the development plans of each district and
see the state of progress of each significant project within a plan
and the country-wide program of each ministry. Frequent briefing
sessions are held with senior government officials to review
progress on the various projects and programs.

Importance of the Private Sector

The great importance of the private sector to Malaysian
development is suggested by the fact that in the Second Five-Year
Plan of Malaya more than half the investment called for was to
come from private sources. As the *Interim Review of
Development in Malaya under the Second Five-Year Plan* says:

> Most of Malaysia's income is produced in the private sector, by small
> farms, rubber estates, tin mines, craftsmen, factories, traders, bankers
> and others. While public investment is doing a great deal to provide
> amenities for living and aids for producing, it is in the private sector
> that we can expect to find most of the immediate sources of our
> needed increases in employment, production and income.
>
> The Second Five-Year Plan set targets for expanding private
> production capacity. The most prominent of these targets concerns
> private investment, that is, private expenditure on plant equipment,
> construction, rubber planting and replanting, and other capital outlays.
> Such targets differ sharply from targets for public investment. While
> public investment is determined by the decision of the federal
> government, the state governments, and the relatively few other public
> authorities, private investment is the result of thousands, even millions,
> of individual business decisions. Government can influence these
> decisions but does not, in most cases, attempt to control them. [2]

Malaysia is unique in its system of "grass roots" plan formulation
and in the attendant means of coordination and review. At the
community level (essentially rural in character) within the 70
districts of Malaya, the private citizen with economic interests
and aspirations has an opportunity to make his views known. But
the district and state development committees and the NDPC do
not have representation from the private industrial or commercial
communities or formal access to the views of the private sector
through advisory bodies associated with them. Although some of
the governmental or quasi-governmental instrumentalities which
have been established to aid in investment have representation
from the private sector, there is no such representation at the
crucial stage in the planning process when broad policies and
goals for development are set.

Pakistan

Officials of state and federal ministries operating in the districts Pakistan became an independent nation in 1947, through the division of the Indian subcontinent. Its two provinces are separated from each other by 1,200 land miles and 3,000 sea miles. They are also radically different in size, population density, topography, resources, and other essential characteristics. Of the 365,000 square miles of Pakistan, only 55,000 are in East Pakistan, but of the total population of approximately 130 million, about 72 million live in East Pakistan. Population density in East Pakistan is 1,200 per square mile; in West Pakistan it is 325. East Pakistan consists largely of delta land and has an agricultural economy, based mainly on rice and jute. West Pakistan has vast areas of desert and semiarid uplands and mountains. Aside from the Indus River basin, West Pakistan's land is suitable only for grazing and limited farming. The binding force bringing these provinces into association is their common Islamic religion.

The geographic separation of the two parts of the country gives Pakistan a uniquely important position in the Muslim world. West Pakistan's situation associates it closely with the oil-rich nations of the Middle East and provides linkages to the Arab-Muslim countries of North Africa. East Pakistan's ties lie in the opposite direction, with the comparatively wealthier countries of southeast Asia, including the Muslim states of Malaysia and Indonesia.

Pakistan, with a high birthrate, high illiteracy, and a low per capita income (about $120 per person in 1969), is one of the poorest countries in the world. Eighty percent of the labor force is engaged in agriculture. About 55 percent of the gross domestic product comes from agriculture; only 15 percent from manufacturing.

Before partition, Pakistan and India had evolved complementary economies: raw jute, cotton, and surplus wheat came from the areas which subsequently formed Pakistan, and jute manufactures, cotton textiles, other manufactured goods, coal, iron, and steel, tobacco, sugar, and other commodities came from India. A goodly proportion of the huge population which moved to India from Pakistan after partition consisted of merchants, businessmen, professionals, office workers, and public administrators. However, the Muslims who came to Pakistan from India were largely poor farmers and craftsmen.

The first decade of the new republic was marked by constitutional difficulties, strife between the two provinces, and mounting economic crises. In 1958 a military regime under General Mohammed Ayub Khan assumed power and abrogated the constitution, dismissed the national and provincial legislative assemblies, and abolished all political parties. Gradually this government, through its efforts to stabilize the economy and because of its evident integrity, won popular confidence. In 1962 a new constitution was adopted that created a federal form of government. It provides for a strong President, with an appointive Council of Ministers, and unicameral national and provincial legislative assemblies. The central government has responsibility for security, international relations, interprovincial affairs, coordination of national economic affairs, and planning and development.

Development Projects

At the time of independence Pakistan had available a stock of development projects that had been prepared before the end of World War II, at the behest of the government of British India, and it also had a Department of Planning and Development which had been set up in anticipation of the end of the war. The new government created the Development Board, to coordinate development plans and to report on the progress of development projects. It also created the Planning Advisory Board, composed of both government officials and representatives of the private sector, which was to promote public cooperation in the development effort. This board was assisted by a group of industrial boards and committees, which set targets for a number of industries. While the government officially supported the idea of planned development, there was not close coordination between it and the Planning Advisory Board in the implementation of projects. For its part, the Board did not prepare a plan but worked on the basis of largely uncoordinated project development.

In 1950, stimulated by the Colombo Plan for Cooperative Economic Development in South and Southeast Asia, Pakistan prepared a six-year development program. This was essentially a public-investment program composed of projects selected with minimal consideration of available resources and the needs of the economy. The fact that it was compiled in three months' time speaks for its limited character as a planning document.

Shortly thereafter, the government reorganized its planning machinery; the Planning Advisory Board was abolished and the Development Board was replaced by the Planning Commission. The Economic Council was also created, with responsibility for implementing the six-year plan. The economic boom attendant upon the Korean War was followed in short order by a decline, creating unpredictable economic conditions in which it was difficult to implement the plan. During this period and in spite of the uncertainties, industrial assets increased three and a half times, partly as a result of increased private investment and partly because of government outlays through the Pakistan Industrial Development Corporation.

In 1953 the government created a new planning board, in the hope of obtaining a better-integrated, five-year plan. However, the board had great difficulty in building an adequate professional staff, and its status vis-à-vis other planning units of the government was not clear. In 1957 it became a permanent agency, and the scope of its responsibilities was enlarged. It was moved to the office of the Prime Minister, who became its chairman. The Secretary of the Ministry of Economic Affairs served as Deputy Chairman and later became Chairman, in place of the Prime Minister.

Especially because of the problem, during this period, of recruiting an able planning staff, the government sought foreign advisory assistance, which was subsequently provided by Harvard University's Development Advisory Service. The advisors aided in the preparation of the First Five-Year Plan (1955-60), trained Pakistanis in the techniques of planning, and conducted or supervised research necessary to the plan preparation.

The results of the First Five-Year Plan were mixed but far from disheartening. It had a great impact on the public in developing an understanding of the importance of planning. It also provided experience in the arduous task of assembling the information needed for plan preparation, and lessons were learned from the failure of important aspects of implementation.

The military government that came into power in 1958 was keenly interested in planning, and it strengthened and enlarged the central planning function. Between 1958 and 1962, when the new Constitution was adopted, various modifications were made in the organizational arrangements for planning. The Government Reorganization Committee, set up to recommend organizational changes called for by the constitution, strongly urged that much planning and implementation be decentralized. Thus, provincial planning and development departments were set up.

In East Pakistan in 1963, a planning board was created with broad planning and evaluation responsibilities. The Planning and Development Department acts as its secretariat. The West Pakistan planning arrangements are approximately the same.

The sectoral sections of the Planning Commission of the central government were strengthened, and an evaluation section was added to assess the results obtained under the total plan. The National Economic Council (NEC) headed by the President, and on which the Provincial Finance Ministers also sit, is responsible for reviewing the country's economic position, the formulation of development plans, and the submission of annual reports to the National Assembly on the progress of the economy. The Secretary of the NEC is the Deputy Chairman of the Planning Commission. The Commission provides the secretariat of the NEC.

The Basic Democracies System

A major effort to move planning and plan implementation to the local level has been inaugurated in recent years, through the system of Basic Democracies. Under this scheme unions are being set up at the local level with responsibility for agricultural, industrial, and community development.

> Voters grouped in units of 1,000 to 1,500 elect ten to twelve members to each council. . . .
> The union councils (town committees in the towns and union committees in the cities) constitute the base of a pyramid consisting in all of five ascending levels of councils each representing larger

geographic units. At the level immediately above the union councils are the *tehsil* (in West Pakistan) or *thana* (in East Pakistan) councils. At the third level are the district councils headed by deputy commissioners or district magistrates, who are civil servants, and, at the fourth, the divisional councils under the chairmanship of divisional commissioners, who are also civil servants. At the top of the pyramid are the two Provincial Development Advisory Councils, headed by the Governor of the Province. Councils at each level send delegates to the councils on the next higher level. . . .

The institutions of Basic Democracies have been assigned both political and economic functions. Their members constitute the Electoral College of Pakistan, which elects the President and the central and provincial legislatures. They are also considered to be organs of local self-government. As such, they have been assigned economic functions which emphasize their responsibility for agricultural, industrial and community development. The Government hopes that they can become the means for decentralizing the preparation and, especially, implementation of plans and for local coordination of development.[3]

The Basic Democracies system, if it is to work, will require technical aid of the kind that is generally not available locally and is in short supply throughout Pakistan. Only if technical skills and development funds can be supplied will such massive decentralization begin to pay off, in the view of the government. It has increasingly been making large sums available to the Basic Democracies units for public works projects.

The Second Five-Year Plan

The work on the Second Five-Year Plan (1960-65) was begun in 1958, building on the foundations laid in the First Plan. The central goals of the plan were to achieve self-sufficiency in food production, improve the balance of trade, and increase employment opportunities for the rapidly expanding labor force. Projects under way were to be continued; new projects were to be considered from several viewpoints: return on investment; foreign-exchange earnings and savings; labor requirements (labor—rather than capital—investment projects being preferred); and locational implications, with special reference to the less developed parts of the country.

The plan relied more heavily on market mechanisms than on direct price and allocation contracts. For example, import restrictions were liberalized. The plan sought to establish a mixed economy, with no industries exclusively reserved for the public sector and with the government concentrating on fields where private capital would not be forthcoming. Both local and foreign private capital were encouraged to invest.

The crucial questions with respect to the effectiveness of the Second Five-Year Plan were, basically, whether agricultural output could be substantially increased, whether steps could be taken to keep the population growth within bounds, and whether foreign aid could be sustained. The expectations with respect to agricultural output have largely been justified, in part because of favorable weather factors. In part, also, the success of the Second Five-Year Plan is attributable to a stable government that strongly backed the plan and concerned itself effectively with the shortages of technical skills and the important organizational and administrative problems.

Because at partition Pakistan lost many civil servants with traditionally skeptical views of the efficacy of private enterprise and also because it possessed so little industry, the government's position has been friendly and encouraging toward the private sector. The fact that industrial growth was phenomenal during the First Plan period was in itself a major factor in stimulating the government to ease controls and to take measures, such as increasing foreign exchange allocations, to aid industry. In addition, faced as it was with a severe shortage of technicians and administrators, the government realized it could not manage an elaborate system of controls and must rely on the market.

The government's position with respect to public and private enterprise was stated in the Second Five-Year Plan:

> It is a basic assumption of the Plan that for the implementation of the industrial development programme, reliance will be placed primarily on private enterprise. This assumption has been made not so much to reduce the burden on public finance as in recognition of the fact that private enterprise has a key role to play in the economic development of the country. Already the development of many industries is directly attributable to private enterprise. During the Plan period the private sector is expected to expand more rapidly. For such expansion, a favorable climate now exists in Pakistan, and conditions are now present for increased private investment, both indigenous and foreign. Price and distribution controls have been relaxed, and this trend is expected to continue. Incentives have been provided to stimulate production and exports. Incentives offered to foreign investors have

been liberalized. Investment treaties and double taxation avoidance agreements calculated to promote private investment have been concluded with a number of countries. Local private enterprise has now acquired a measure of experience and know-how which qualifies it to expand its operation either independently or in collaboration with foreign investors.

In several sectors of industry the choice may well arise between public and private enterprise. The cardinal principle is that there should be no public industrial sector in the sense of reservation of complete industries for public enterprise, but that the Government should remain generally responsible for promoting all industries by providing the required facilities and should directly participate only in those enterprises which are essential for overall development and where private capital is not forthcoming or high considerations of national security intervene.[4]

Private initiative has been particularly active in the textile, jute-processing, and sugar-refining fields. Important expansion has taken place in the steel industry with the initiation of National Steel of Pakistan, a private corporation begun by several Pakistani industrialists. Private commercial banking and insurance are becoming more important.

Banks are mainly concentrated in the larger towns and handle mostly nonagricultural loans. The government is stimulating the insurance business by granting tax concessions and by reinsurance activity through its Pakistan Insurance Corporation. The Karachi Stock Exchange was founded in 1949, and the Dacca Exchange in 1956. Few companies have as yet offered capital stock to the public, but this form of investment is expanding.

When Ayub Khan took over the government in 1958, there were over 1,000 local organizations representing business and private industry. In 1961 the government reorganized these groups and established a licensing system. The central agency that speaks for business and industry is now the Federation of Pakistan Chambers of Commerce and Industry. Affiliated with it are 11 major chambers of commerce and industry for 11 geographic areas and 48 associations that represent specific industries on a nationwide basis. There are also smaller town associations and regional trade groups.

The role of business and industry in the actual preparation of the Second Plan was modest. Following approval by the Economic Council of the *Outline of the Second Five-Year Plan*, it was widely circulated within the central and provincial governments and among private groups. The Planning Commission requested comments from the chambers of commerce and industry and from trade and labor associations during the review. But during the preparation phase, the responsibility for developing proposals for the private sector rested mainly with the central ministries and provincial governments, and they were able to submit only limited information. This was especially true with regard to industry in East Pakistan. As a result, the Planning Commission undertook to work out the programs for industry itself. It assembled panels of representatives from the private sector, but their effectiveness in producing useful data and proposals appears to have been limited. Thus, while business and industry were able to submit opinions on the *Outline*, not much of their knowledge, experience, and judgment were fed into its preparation. This situation reflected the fact that the planning processes in Pakistan were still evolving and maturing and that the mobilization of the private sector's resources for participation in plan preparation was still only partially achieved.

Iran

Iran is the fourth largest producer of oil in the world, exceeded only by the United States, Russia, and Venezuela. Its oil revenues put it in a highly favorable position with respect to development, providing better than one third of the funds necessary for development programs and making its balance of payments situation relatively easy.

Its population is about 22 million, and although the birth rate has always been high (about 45 per thousand), its mortality rate is also high, and given the size of the country (about one fifth that of the United States), it has a relatively low overall population density. It is one of the very few developing nations in which population growth is not a problem.

Under the Constitution of 1960, as subsequently amended, the government is composed of the National Consultation Assembly, or Majlis, and the Senate. The Majlis is elective, the members representing towns or districts on a population basis. The Senate has half of its membership chosen by popular vote, half appointed by the Shah. The Shah names the Prime Minister. Legislation may be introduced by members of either house or by the Prime Minister and the ministries. The Shah has the right of absolute veto.

The Constitution has been assessed as being more an arbiter between the executive and legislative branches than an elucidation of the fundamental relationships between a people and its government. The basic fact of Iranian government is still, in spite of the Constitution, the dominant position of the Shah.

Nearly 80 percent of the Iranian population are in the agricultural sector, although only about one tenth of the land is used for agriculture. Most of the country lacks adequate rainfall, and the soil is generally poor. Land ownership has been concentrated in the hands of absentee landlords and religious institutions, as well as the Crown. In recent years the royal estates have been broken up and sold to peasant cooperatives, under the direct leadership of the Shah, in an effort to encourage land redistribution. Only about 2 percent of the working force are engaged in industry and at least half of this is of the cottage variety. The making of carpets, hand-loom weaving, and other home crafts are a major aspect of the very limited industrial picture.

In the 1920's, under the leadership of Reza Khan, the government encouraged private enterprise by facilitating the import of capital equipment, providing tariff protection, and entering directly into industrial development. In 1946, the present Shah created the Industrial and Mining Bank, to operate enterprises formerly controlled by various government ministries, as well as to encourage new development. The Bank also performed general banking functions and furnished technical assistance to private industry. It was liquidated in 1949, and its operations were taken over by the government's Plan Organization, which was created to operate the new seven-year plan for economic development.

Economic Planning

Although a group of American experts, the Millspaugh Mission, proposed a number of economic and fiscal measures in the 1920's that looked toward the planned development of Iran, it was not until the 1930's that tentative efforts at economic planning began. In 1937, for example, a trade council made up of government officials indicated that its principal responsibility would be to prepare an economic plan for the country. But it was disbanded without accomplishing this objective.

After World War II a commission within the Ministry of Finance drafted a plan for government-development expenditures for a seven-year period. While substantial foreign reserves had been accumulated during the war years, these were inadequate to finance the proposed expenditures, so the government applied to the International Bank for Reconstruction and Development for a loan. It was informed that loans could only be made for projects whose feasibility had been demonstrated through technical studies. An American engineering firm was brought in to make the studies. It recommended three alternative levels of programs, each with a set of feasible projects. The Cabinet and Parliament subsequently created the Plan Organization, to carry through the recommended proposals. It was this organization that took over the activities of the Industrial and Mining Bank.

The Plan Organization was given broad powers not only to exercise supervision of the seven-year plan but to execute projects itself. It was allocated substantial oil revenues, and thus had resources at its command for development purposes. Since the plan was really a collection of individual projects that had been prepared after only limited study and with little consultation between the ministries and agencies, the Plan Organization employed a second engineering firm to provide continuing technical services. In late 1951, because of the dispute between the Anglo-Iranian Oil Company and the government of Prime Minister Mossadegh, oil revenues virtually ceased. The dispute was not resolved until 1954, and the seven-year plan never got much beyond paper.

In that year, the Parliament, foreseeing the availability of oil revenues as well as an opportunity for foreign loans and loans from the Bank Melli, the government-owned commercial bank of Iran, requested the Plan Organization to develop and execute a second seven-year plan.

Many problems confronted the planning agency at this juncture, some inherent in the mandate given to it and some derivative from the nature of Iranian society and organization. For example, giving the Plan Organization responsibility for executing development projects made sense in view of the fact that the regular ministries and agencies lacked the competence required for a major development effort. But to give the Plan Organization the major task of execution was to ask that it virtually create a new machinery of government. Nor were conditions in general especially conducive to success for the Plan Organization. There was no clear-cut source of power committed to development. The Shah's position was equivocal. The bureaucracy was weak in quality, excessive in quantity. At the top of civil service, changes of key personnel were the order of the day. Government was so highly centralized in Teheran as to make effective field operations most difficult.

The Second Plan, like the first, was primarily a collection of projects, largely uncoordinated. It did not include estimates of public sector expenditures or of private expenditures. It contained no comprehensive set of economic policies. Foreign consulting firms were brought in to supervise most of the road program and the port and airport programs. The results, on the whole, were not spectacular. There were exceptions, however. The multipurpose regional development schemes in the Moghan plains, in the Kuzestan Province, and in the Sistan-Baluchistan desert area were put in the hands of foreign consultants, who did the physical construction of dams, plants, experimental stations, etc. They also developed the administrative machinery to operate the installations and trained Iranians to take over their operation. This approach seemed to work with great success.

The Third Plan

In 1960 the Plan Organization began preparing the Third Plan, to go into effect in 1962. It undertook, first, a review of the results of the Second Plan and reached two important conclusions:

...The planning and execution of most programmes involve more than one public agency. The divided responsibility and often independent policy pursued by these agencies have led in many instances to confusion, waste and duplication. Better programming is needed in the various government agencies concerned with development, as well as coordination of their programmes with those of the Plan Organization.

Closely related to the problem of coordination is the need for taking a comprehensive view of the size of the total development effort and its relation to the economic objectives of the plan and to the private as well as the public sectors. Therefore the "Program Review" concludes that in formulating the Third Plan, the problem of economic development should be approached from the viewpoint of national objectives and the total volume of finance needed to attain them.[5]

The Division of Economic Affairs of the Plan Organization took the leadership in formulating the outline of the Third Plan. One unit of the Division worked on an analysis of the objectives of and resources for the plan. Functional committees were established, with representatives of the Division sitting on them, to bring together relevant ministries and agencies for the development of sectional or functional programs. On the basis of this effort, the *Outline of the Third Plan, 1341-1346 (September 1962-March 1968)* was prepared. Its method of procedure represented progress on two important fronts: it involved the ministries and agencies in the planning process, and it put the plan into a national economic framework.

The Third Plan, running from September 1962 to March 1968, has as its goal increasing the national income by a yearly average of 6 percent, the rate of growth at the end of the Second Plan. Developmental expenditures were estimated for the Third Plan at about the same level as those at the end of the Second Plan, with an annual increase of 6 percent projected for the plan period. The distribution of development expenditures between the public and the private sectors was based on experience in the Second Plan.

The Third Plan relies heavily on the expansion of the private sector. It stresses, on the agricultural front, extension services, small irrigation and well projects, and access roads. It makes important recommendations with regard to manpower development, statistical services, and the mobilization of municipal services. It proposes strengthening the planning bureaus in the ministries by providing them with expert staffs and by setting up a program to train planners.

The planning experience of Iran, to date, is illustrative of the evolution that many of the developing nations are going through as they learn about the modes and requirements of sensible plan preparation and execution. It represents a common experience in its struggle to find the most suitable organizational arrangements for planning; in its giving the Plan Organization responsibility for both planning and execution and subsequently arriving at the conclusion that the government's ministries and agencies must participate in the processes of planning and implementation and must be given adequate machinery to do so; in its realization that unrationalized and uncoordinated collections of projects do not add up to a development plan and that a plan must be set within the framework of national resources and requirements; in its growing awareness that annual budgets must bear a close relationship to annual objectives under the longer-range plan; and in its realization of the data and manpower weaknesses at its command.

The principal immediate problem for private industry in Iran is obtaining credit. This issue had been addressed in a number of ways. For example, in 1959 the Industrial and Mining Development Bank (IMDBI), the country's first private investment house, was set up in part through a substantial interest-free advance from the government. The objectives of the IMDBI are to mobilize private savings and other domestic financial resources and to channel them to industrial, mining, and transportation enterprises. It also seeks to attract foreign technical and managerial skills, as well as capital, to these enterprises. In addition to the IMDBI there are two other private banks and several government-owned banks, including the Bank Melli Iran (the National Bank), and agricultural, export development, development, and industrial credit banks.

Under the Third Plan, given the good showing of industry in the preceding plan period, more emphasis was placed on industrial development particularly in fields where Iran has taken advantages in terms of raw materials, skills, and domestic or foreign market potentialities. For example, cotton textiles increased 600 percent between 1955 and 1961; cement 468 percent; oil 337 percent;

soaps 247 percent. Stress was placed on small- and medium-sized industries, and priorities were given to those having a favorable effect on the balance of payments and those supplying essential consumer goods. Sixty percent of the investment under the Third Plan's program for industrialization was to come from the private sector.

Role of Private Industry

Two statements from the *Outline of the Third Plan* indicate the government's position with respect to the role of private industry:

> The government will promote industrial growth primarily through credit funds earmarked for specific types of private investments, and through a few direct investments of its own. The earmarked credits will consist of funds for distribution of approved institutions such as the Industrial and Mining Development Bank and the Industrial Credit Bank for the purposes described in the plan. The government will use direct investment (i.e., building government-owned plants) only for larger industrial and mining projects and after it is determined that no qualified private investors are interested. . . .
>
> The increase in private investment during the second plan period has been so promising that the government has so far felt that it should not enter into direct industrial investment unless private investors do not enter fields considered essential to industrial development. Experience with government-owned factories in Iran shows that, as a general rule, from a commercial point of view they are not efficiently managed, although technically they may be operated with greater competence. This approach to industrial investment is non-doctrinaire and will be modified in the light of the climate for industrial development in the country.[6]

The important role assigned to the private sector in the industrial development of the country under the Third Plan is in contrast to the small amount of direct participation of business and industry in its preparation. None of the concern expressed in the *Outline of the Third Plan* for engaging the ministries and agencies in the planning process seems to have been extended to the private sector.

As early as 1954, 20 chambers of commerce were formally recognized in 20 geographic districts of Iran. Their purpose was and is to transmit opinions from the private business, commercial, and industrial community to the Ministry of Commerce and other government officials. They are partially supported by government funds. In 1955 the Chamber of Industry was formed, which permitted industries, as such, to be represented. Thus, the mechanisms exist for bringing private experience, judgments, and data to bear on the planning process. However, the only evidence of participation in the preparation of the Third Plan was limited advisory assistance to some of the sectoral planning committees.

In this respect, Iran is like a number of other countries that are eager to industrialize, are willing to give to the private sector an important role in the development plan and process, and look on private entrepreneurship with a favorable, even friendly, eye. They nonetheless do not involve at the crucial stage of planning those nongovernmental individuals and organizations whose judgment and support is needed in the setting of goals, targets, and priorities. This would appear to be the next important procedural step to be taken in strengthening the methods of planning.

The Philippines

The Philippines appears to be both the most and the least likely of the modernizing countries to be concerned with planning and the role of the private sector. Its composition, thousands of islands in a giant archipelago; its rapidly growing population of more than 30 million; its basically agricultural and farm-product-oriented economy—all would seem to argue the need for strong governmental leadership to effect successful modernization. But at the same time, its geographical dispersion and its close identity with American economic interests and values would seem to inhibit explicit planning—particularly insofar as the private sector is concerned. The Philippine story is clearly a mixed and complicated one. The country has a sense of nationhood, derived from its colonial past under Spain and from the unifying force of the Catholic Church. Later, American domination meant the introduction of relatively uncontrolled and exploitative free enterprise; but it also meant progressive steps toward self-government and the development of a substantial educated population.

The Republic of the Philippines came into existence in 1946. Its constitution, at least superficially, resembles that of the

United States. Presidential powers, to begin with, have been extended in practice so that the Presidency is clearly the dominant branch of government. Strong leadership is in the cultural tradition of the Filipinos and is accepted readily. The President has wide powers of appointment, and he has supervisory control over local governments. As chief administrator, he issues executive orders to effectuate legislative measures and can thus put his own image on the policies enacted by the Congress. He has an item veto over revenue and tariff bills.

Citizen participation in politics is extensive. Filipinos like politics and enjoy the political process. The culture has led them to see relationships as personal, to view associations in terms of the status of participants, and to expect a quid pro quo for every service performed. This, in part, has resulted in a willingness to use political institutions for bargaining purposes and has made possible an environment in which give and take are characteristic. At its best, this cultural situation encourages political decisions which serve larger, rather than individual, interests and suggests hopeful possibilities for consensus politics.

World War II produced profound changes in the Philippines. Although the devastation of the country was great and production declined drastically, a new class of entrepreneurs emerged, many of whom took advantage of wartime scarcities and the opportunity to deal in surplus goods in the immediate postwar period. They depended in part on political help to carry out commercial activities and began to develop an awareness of the political process and its utilities.

That the Philippines appear definitely committed to democratic political institutions seems clear. Growing literacy and economic sophistication characterize the society and there is an expanding middle class, the product of urbanization, industrialization, and general economic growth. An expanding institutional structure of rural banks and credit corporations, life insurance companies, and postal-savings institutions encourages savings. Foreign investment, especially from the United States, continues to be available, and Japanese reparations and loans can be counted on for nearly 20 years ahead. The "normalization" of Philippine commercial policy is having the effect of channeling revenues to the government which can be used for social investment. Finally, the stability of the Philippine economy in postwar years is encouraging investors, both foreign and domestic.

In 1962, almost immediately after taking office, the Macapagal administration devalued the peso and moved toward ending controls. This has allowed the more enterprising industries to expand and, given the limited Philippine domestic market, is encouraging a new interest in the market possibilities of Southeast Asia.

Development Plans

Since the end of the war, numerous development plans have been formulated and several planning agencies created. In 1946 and 1947 various programs were proposed for government expenditures for development purposes. One was the Beyster Plan, which set forth a somewhat grandiose list of projects, mostly of an industrial nature. In 1947 the Philippine-United States Agricultural Mission presented an estimate of agricultural needs and resources. A 12-year electric power program was announced by the government. Also in 1947, the National Economic Council was reorganized and charged with the duties of advising the President on economic policy and coordinating government expenditures.

In 1948 the Cuaderno Plan for the period 1949-53 was presented, estimating for the first time the sources of development funds. From 1950 to 1953, the Philippine Commission for United States Aid, PHILCUSA, developed lists of projects and economic targets. PHILCUSA was guided by the Bell Mission, which advocated that the role of the central government in economic development should be limited to the provision of infrastructure, social services, and credit facilities. At the time, the government owned several industrial and utility enterprises.

In 1954 the National Economic Council (NEC) presented a five-year plan for the period 1955-59. It concentrated on means of increasing employment and proposed to rely on the private sector for industrial growth. Also in 1954, Republic Act No. 1000 was passed, providing for government bond issues to finance development projects. Act No. 1000 expenditures were not made in accordance with the five-year plan or any preceding plans, but they strengthened the economic base of the country by initiating capital investment in industry and transportation.

In the same year, the Government Survey and Reorganization Commission advocated more effective central planning procedures. In 1956 President Magsaysay reorganized the NEC, which in the next year presented a five-year plan for the period 1957-61. This was very comprehensive and utilized advanced analytic techniques. It did not affect the Act No. 1000 expenditures. It never received congressional sanction, and its implementation was fragmentary.

An executive order in 1957 established the Budget Commission, headed by the Fiscal Policy Council, composed of the Secretary of Finance, the Budget Commissioner, the Governor of the Central Bank, and the Chairman of the NEC. By preparing fiscal plans and annual budget proposals apart from the five-year plan of the NEC, this agency became in fact the planning unit for the government. The NEC, politically isolated and associated with U.S. aid missions, had little influence in the legislature. Few powers were available to it for guiding the private sector toward the development goals of the plan. The Budget Commission and the Central Bank were much more influential in the allocation of government expenditures. Direct public participation in the economy was discredited by the inefficiency of the government industrial enterprises and marketing boards. For these reasons, government incentives and subsidies were made on an ad hoc basis, as were the Act No. 1000 expenditures. United States aid was also on a project basis. During the late 1950's it was U.S. policy not to tie aid expenditures to any long-range planning, including the NEC plan.

Upon taking office in January 1962, President Macapagal announced the Five-Year Integrated Socio-Economic Program for 1963-67. The basic philosophy of the program was that economic growth must be pursued in order to answer the needs of the growing population and its aspirations for a higher standard of living. It conceived of the task of economic development as belonging principally to private enterprise, maintaining that the government should not go "into business" and that the government "can never become a good businessman." The program saw the government's role as being one of assisting the private sector and providing it with guidance toward economic growth. It maintained that the operations of the private sector depend upon the government's plans and policies, which should be clear-cut, stable, and not subject to drastic changes.

The Macapagal Program, which eclipsed the NEC's Three-Year Program, was presented to the Congress in January 1962. In August of that year, President Macapagal created the Program Implementation Agency, to do economic policy research and to help implement its Five-Year Socio-Economic Program.

The Philippine private sector did not participate in the preparation of President Macapagal's Five-Year Socio-Economic Program, which was the product of the President's own advisors and of foreign technical experts. The private sector appeared to be less concerned with the development policies proposed by the President than with actions taken by the Congress and expressed itself largely through the Congress. When the Marcos administration came into office in 1966, it promulgated a new development program of its own. This was prepared hastily and apparently without consultation with the private sector.

Agencies Involved in Development

Several agencies are involved in relationships between government development planning and the private sector. One is the Development Bank of the Philippines, which in 1958 took over the agricultural financing activity of the Rehabilitation Finance Corporation. It now has extended its financing to industrial projects and can be expected to play a major part in implementing the industrialization targets of recent administrations. The Emergency Employment Administration, the National Cottage Industrial Development Administration, and the Agricultural Credit Cooperative Finance Administration are instrumental in influencing the private sector toward the goals of the government.

The Mindanao Development Authority (MDA), established in June 1961 by Republic Act No. 3034, is a regional development effort. The purpose of MDA is to stimulate the creation of new industrial and agricultural activity on the relatively undeveloped island of Mindanao. It is extending financial, management, and technical support to new industrial and agricultural enterprises. It coordinates the various public and private entities involved in implementing development projects.

The MDA came into being partly as a result of the interest of a private citizens' group, the Mindanao-Sulu-Palawan Association, which in 1959 began to press for a public authority that would stimulate investment in the Mindanao region. The MDA was conceived as a third sector, or coordinating body, which would not replace or duplicate the functions of such agencies as the National Resettlement and Rehabilitation Administration and the Department of Commerce and Industry. The MDA may borrow funds, purchase or dispose of its shares of capital, and exercise the right of eminent domain. Its operations are, for the most part, tax exempt.

The MDA was initially capitalized at 30 million pesos, and 30 million pesos have been added annually for the first nine years of its operation. The private sector contributed approximately 40 percent of the capital investment in Mindanao over the 1962-66 period. In order to attract this level of investment, the MDA has been providing marketing assistance, exemptions, and subsidies and is aiding in the development of transportation and other infrastructure facilities.

A national agency of potential significance is the National Planning Commission. This organization is responsible for building codes, subdivision regulations, and other aspects of urban and regional planning of a physical nature. It is charged with the responsibility of preparing physical development plans on urban, regional, and national scales. Despite its broad mandate, it has to date concentrated mostly on building and land subdivision regulations. Its planning activity is not coordinated with that of the National Economic Council or the Program Implementation Agency, which was renamed the Presidential Economic Staff by President Marcos. However, since all private economic activity has a physical or locational dimension, it is an agency which potentially could have great influence on the private sector, especially in newly developing regions.

Notes

1. Clair Wilcox, *The Planning and Execution of Economic Development in Southeast Asia*, Occasional Papers in International Affairs, No. 10, (Cambridge, Mass.: Center for International Affairs, Harvard University, January 1965), pp. 25-26.

2. Malaysia, *Interim Review of Development in Malaya under the Second Five-Year Plan* (Kuala Lumpur, December 1963), p. 35.

3, Albert Waterston, *Planning in Pakistan: Organization and Implementation* (Baltimore: The Johns Hopkins Press, for the Economic Development Institute, 1963), pp. 94-95.

4. Pakistan, *The Second Five-Year Plan, 1960-1965, Including Revised Estimates* (Karachi: Planning Commission, 1961), pp. 225-26.

5. Iran, *Outline of the Third Plan, 1341-1346 (September 1962-March 1968)* (Teheran: Plan Organization, 1342 (1963)), p. 20.

6. *Ibid.*, pp. 92, 96-97.

4 Conclusions

By way of summary comment, certain generalizations may be highlighted, restating some of the quite apparent, as well as some of the less obvious, propositions.

First, of course, is the uniqueness of each country's situation and the necessity, thus imposed, of adapting to the particular environment any approach, system, or scheme that appears instructive for those concerned with drawing the private sector more effectively into the planning process. The tools and concepts of economic analysis, *e.g.*, statistical series and GNP, are more generally applicable in any environment than are the tools and concepts of administration. This is a point not always fully appreciated.

Second is the fact that many of the modernizing nations have numerous characteristics in common, which provide, to a degree, environmental circumstances that are conducive to the transfer of experience. All place great expectations in industrialization and most are, by the standards of the so-called developed nations, in an early stage of industrial growth. All are characterized by low per capita incomes and high dependence on agriculture. Most possess limited resources of skilled manpower. Most have shortages of capital. Many are classical "colonial" nations, with economies based on the export of raw materials and the import of manufactures. Political instability resulting from internal dissension or external threat is a lurking problem for most.

Third is the widespread evidence that planning is an evolutionary and experimental phenomenon in virtually all the countries under examination. Only in the case of India has the commitment to planning been so deep and pervasive as to make it essentially a basic element of the governmental structure.

Elsewhere, government planning has been approached reluctantly and almost negatively, as in the Philippines; in an off-again, on-again manner, as in Iran; or when embraced enthusiastically, as in Malaysia, Pakistan, and Tunisia, as an important outgrowth of achieving political stability. In some cases, the route to national planning appears to be through regional planning, such as the Philippines' MDA.

The significance, for our purposes, of the evolutionary and experimental nature of planning in most countries is that there is considerable opportunity for the role of the private sector to undergo change and development. If the private sector is not given an opportunity to contribute its judgments, knowledge, and factual resources to the earliest phases of plan-making, this does not mean that a more significant role may not be played in the future. Indeed, if the Indian experience is suggestive, even the most doctrinaire views on planning as essentially a governmental function are gradually being modified to permit an earlier and more significant contribution from the private sector.

Fourth, there is considerable evidence that governmental planning serves as a valuable instrument in nation-building. It is being used for this purpose in Tanzania, Malaysia, and Pakistan. Undoubtedly, as arrangements are perfected for involvement of the private sector, industrial and agricultural, the utility of planning in molding a national consciousness will increase.

Fifth, the agents of private-sector representation do not automatically exist or may be of limited utility because they represent narrow or antiquated views. Some nations have had to take the initiative in creating instruments of consultation, *e.g.*, Turkey, Malaysia, and Pakistan. Others have found that the associations which might speak for industry and agriculture do so with the voices of the *ancien régime*. This has led in the case of Chile to the Frei government's encouraging the selection of new agents to express the views of the private community.

Sixth, it seems clear that the determination of when and how the outlook of the private sector will be introduced into the planning process, thereby encouraging a genuinely productive relationship, is a delicate matter that must take due account of the general public interest. In some societies the ethics of the private community do not preclude taking advantage of privileged knowledge for personal gain. In others, where ethical standards are more rigorous, the public expects institutional arrangements that will assure protection of the common interest. Obviously, in every country the spokesmen for the nation are the head of government and his chief associates. Thus, while all reasonable efforts need to be made to encourage a significant role for the private sector, limits must be imposed to prevent abuse of its access to information or its influence. Ultimately, government alone must make certain planning judgments and decisions. What is crucial is that these be informed by the desires, experience, and knowledge of all parts of the community and that, in turn, the community be provided with an understanding of the reasons for governmental policies to the maximum extent possible. In this connection, governments need to make clear, as many in fact have done, their "philosophical" position with regard to the role of the private sector in development. In addition, governments should be willing to reappraise, from time to time, their doctrinal stances. Ideology can both inspire and stultify, as the Indian planning experience seems to indicate. Clearly, it is less important to preserve doctrine than to encourage socioeconomic development.

As has been seen, the devices used for private-sector participation vary considerably. Most frequently, the unions of chambers of commerce and industry offer a handy means of communicating industrial and business viewpoints, as do the federations of labor the workers' position. Having industrial representation on the central planning council may be a useful approach, although the employment of advisory committees from industry to provide guidance to the council may be a more appropriate means of keeping government's ultimate responsibility clear. Extensive local participation, as in Malaysia, is valuable in carrying awareness of socioeconomic needs and interests upward from the people to the planners. But if depended on exclusively, local voices provide little sense of the main thrusts of private interest in the nation. Most countries, it would appear, need to work at developing and experimenting with the instruments of private-sector participation. They also need to experiment with how and when the private sector should be brought into the planning process. If the conviction exists, as it does in most nations, that this is a matter of importance, viable arrangements will almost certainly begin to emerge from the experimentation.

Part 2 Policies and Programs to Encourage Private-Sector Performance in Accordance with Planned Goals

5   Amassing and Allocation of Capital

Introduction

The private sector, including private agricultural activity, accounts for a very high percentage of the national income of most modernizing countries (about 90 percent in India, for example). Although participation in the preparation of national plans on the part of the private sector is in most situations marginal at best, there are few nations without programs designed to encourage industrial development more or less in the direction of plan targets. Little distinction seems to be drawn between industrialization under indigenous and under foreign leadership, although a number of programs are specifically designed to encourage or aid one or the other. Limits are sometimes set on the extent of foreign participation, but industrialization per se is generally the goal, since it is so widely accepted by most developing countries as a key to modernization.

The measures adopted by governments serve both government and industry; sometimes they are frustrating to one but necessary from the viewpoint of the other. From the governmental outlook, expansion of industry tends to be a prime objective because of its beneficial consequences for employment, its contribution to improved per capita income and increased standards of living, its utilization of the nation's natural resources, and its contributions, direct or otherwise, to military strength and political stability.

Industrialization can occur only if there are capital resource:
available, so governments concern themselves with the capita
market, with savings and savings institutions, with developmen
loan banks and funds, with foreign loans, and with aid-in-kind
that may serve as a capital substitute. Since a governmenta
obligation is to keep solvent at home and abroad and to achieve
development while maintaining balance in the economy, there is
interest on the part of governments in controlling imports of
foreign capital, in keeping allocations of resources for capita
development within manageable limits in terms of anticipated
revenues and borrowings, and in keeping prices and wage:
relatively stable. Beyond this, governments may regulate new
investment through licensing or other means, to assure that
wherever possible domestic enterprises move into fields which wil
allow for substitution of imports to reduce pressure on
balance-of-payments accounts. Labor-intensive enterprises may be
favored, and encouragement given to firms that locate in areas of
high unemployment or areas designated for special developmen
attention. The stimulation of small-scale industry is especially
significant for regional and local development purposes. Firms
that are able to utilize existing or planned infrastructure, that are
able to use but do not exceed in their requirements available
supplies of power, and firms that employ locally available raw
materials and other goods and services may be favored.
Governments, in their interest in earning foreign exchange, may
undertake to assist in quality control of products and may make
market surveys and conduct export promotion drives. They may,
in a few instances, support or encourage research as a route to
new industrial development.

The interests and requirements of new or expanding industries
may parallel those of government. But the individual firm's ability
to survive economically is paramount. Thus, the likelihood of
profitability and the possibilities of favorable tax arrangements
and tariff protection from foreign competition, especially during
the period of initial establishment, are most important. The
availability of capital at favorable rates, of essential infrastructure
(power, transportation facilities, plant), of managerial talent, and
of labor that is trained or amenable to training, is of great
interest. The nature of the market for the firm's products and the

existence of market surveys and export promotion activities are also significant. Perhaps above all in importance is the reading which the entrepreneur makes of the "climate of opportunity." Is a given situation one in which the government is reasonably stable, clearly sympathetic to private entrepreneurship, and likely to encourage, rather than harass and limit, economic expansion? The specific arrangements employed by governments to encourage industrial development in line with planned objectives are considered in the following pages. The discussion does not attempt to categorize all of the arrangements used in each country but, rather, indicates, through selective illustration, the variety of possibilities.

Amassing Capital

The accumulation of capital for development is difficult for any modernizing society. For nations which give allegiance to free and open political, social, and economic institutions, it is particularly complex, since rigorous measures to enforce savings and to build up capital tend not to be acceptable. Russian capital for development was generated in substantial part from the forced savings of workers and peasants, through imposing very low levels of income and consumption during the first decades after the Revolution. Much more moderate measures are employed in other types of societies.

The ensuing very partial discussion of methods of mobilizing individual savings for development purposes suggests useful approaches to capital accumulation, but it does not consider a variety of other means of amassing capital. Important among these, for example, are foreign grants and loans, the opportunities for which are generally well-known and widely used.

India

Table 1 shows the sources of domestic financing of government-development outlays in India's Third Five-Year Plan and is suggestive of the approaches taken in non-Communist countries.

TABLE 1

Indian Third Five-Year Plan
Domestic Financing of Government Development

	Item	Outlay in crores
(1)	Balance from current revenues (excluding additional taxation)	550
(2)	Contribution of railways	100
(3)	Surpluses of other public enterprises	450
(4)	Loans from the public (net)	800
(5)	Small savings (net)	600
(6)	Provident funds (net), steel equalization fund, and balance of miscellaneous capital receipts over non-Plan disbursements	540
(7)	Additional taxation, including results of new policies to increase surplus of public enterprises	1,710
(8)	Budgetary receipts corresponding to external assistance	2,200
(9)	Deficit financing	550
(10)	TOTAL	7,500

* One crore equals 10 million rupees.

Source: Adapted from John P. Lewis, *Quiet Crisis in India* (Washington: The Brookings Institution, 1962), p. 103.

Personal savings are significant in the total development scheme, both as a source of capital and as an antiinflationary measure. Most countries encourage private savings through the inauguration of new savings schemes. In India, under the Third Plan, emphasis was placed on increasing private savings through the elaborate national network of cooperatives, which act as savings banks. A second "savings" institution is the Life Insurance Corporation of India, which is nationalized—the only insurance company in the country and the largest single institutional investor.

Pakistan

In Pakistan, as a means of "mopping up" private savings that have not found their way into commercial banks or other capital-accumulating institutions, the Industrial Redevelopment Bank is permitted to accept deposits. The Agricultural Development Bank, organized as successor to the Agricultural Development Corporation and the Agricultural Bank, is also empowered to accept deposits. Postal savings are an increasingly important means of private saving in Pakistan.

Malaysia

In Malaysia a major source of development capital is the Employers' Provident Fund. The Malayan Fund, which has about a million and a half contributors, is able to provide more than $100 million annually in long-term loans to the government, and about 60 percent of the public long-term domestic debt comes from this source. This type of saving supplements Post Office savings, insurance company funds, and commercial bank deposits as assets to be drawn upon for development capital.

The Philippines

The Philippines Government Service Insurance System, which operates a retirement plan for civil servants, invests over 30 percent of its assets in government securities, providing an important source for development capital. Insurance companies, commercial banks, rural banks, postal savings, and a securities exchange are also significant development capital sources in the Philippines.

Allocation of Capital

The Philippines

The arrangements used by governments for the allocation of capital for development are extensive and varied. The Philippines has had a central bank since 1949, of which one function is "to promote a rising level of production, employment and real income in the Philippines." It also has broad powers over the country's entire banking system. The Philippine National Bank, which was established in 1916 with the government providing most of the capitalization, has created a subsidiary, the National Investment and Development Corporation, which processes loans for chemical, steel, agricultural, engineering, mineral and hotel operations.

The Development Bank of the Philippines was founded in 1959, as successor to the postwar Rehabilitation Finance Corporation. It finances agricultural and industrial enterprises and aids the formation of rural and private development banks. It also guarantees foreign investment loans to Philippine industry.

An extensive system of commercial banks (36 in number) operates throughout the Philippines. While these banks have, in the past, been traditionally cautious with respect to longer-term loans for industrial development, they have been encouraged in this direction by the Central Bank, with a consequent substantial increase in industrial loans during the past decade.

In 1963, the private Development Corporation of the Philippines was established with a combination of share capital, a loan from the United States Agency for International Development, and a substantial credit line from the World Bank. The specific purpose in creating the Corporation was to fill the gap between demand and supply of long-term capital for industry. Its approved loans have been in such fields as chemicals, food processing, ceramics, glass-making, steel, mining, fisheries, transport, and electric utilities. Not untypically, a deterrent to a greater volume of favorable loan actions than at present by the Corporation is the absence of well-planned projects that are both technically and financially feasible.

Malaysia

In Malaysia, banking and other institutions concerned with funding for industrial development are going though a process of change. Malaysia, like the Philippines, was primarily a trading country, and its banking system had been concerned with financing the movement of goods in and out of the country and with loans to existing mining and plantation companies. The creation of a central bank in 1958 was for the purpose of giving the government of Malaya a means of controlling and directing, as necessary, existing banking institutions and of assuring adequate banking facilities to the government. The Central Bank of Malaya is now evolving into an institution to serve the whole of Malaysia. Its earlier operation is suggestive of the kind of role it is now able to play. It is responsible for controlling the credits granted by private banks and has followed the practice, in concert with the Treasury, of convening conferences of bankers to brief them on future development needs and associated government policies. In 1961, for example, private banks were asked to pursue a more selective credit line, and were advised of the priorities under the Second Five-Year Development Plan that should be considered.

In the mid-1950's, the International Bank for Reconstruction and Development proposed the creation of a new industrial credit institution, and in 1960 a public company, the Malayan Industrial Development Finance, Ltd. (MIDFL), was set up with the Central Bank represented on its Board. The share capital of MIDFL was to be held by the federal government, the main exchange banks, insurance companies, the Commonwealth Development Corporation, and the Commonwealth Development Finance Company. The MIDFL offers both long- and medium-term (10- to 15-year) loans and provides other banking as well as advisory services. Its policies have been conservative. Given limited resources, it has invested in first-class securities and put the resulting revenues into new developments. This, in effect, means lending initially to those who are already established. The range of its services of significance to industrial development are described in its publication *Capital for Industry:*

1. Advisory services in regard to raising capital.

2. Medium- or long-term loans, with MIDFL willing to supply up to half of the total fixed capital required for a new or existing project.

3. Debenture, preference or equity share participation in public or private companies, with the ultimate expectation that MIDFL will dispose of its holdings.

4. Factory mortgage finance for the purchase of factory buildings, with up to 80 percent of the cost on long-term easy repayment loans. MIDFL has a variety of standard factory units available to assist in achieving well-designed structures.

5. Hire-purchase finance to assist in the financing of machines and equipment, which MIDFL will supply.

6. Shares can be issued by MIDFL to raise capital for new and existing companies and it can underwrite capital issues.

7. MIDFL maintains a group of "turnkey" projects, which are ready-made plans for the complete establishment of production units. The plans include descriptions of capital cost, plant layout, equipment and labor requirements. They also include provisions for on-site technical assistance by the suppliers of machinery as well as suitable credit facilities.[1]

Another financing institution in Malaysia, the Commonwealth Development Corporation (CDC), is financed with borrowings from the British Treasury. It is managed from London and operates through six regional offices, one of which is located in Malaysia. It functions on a strictly commercial basis, putting some funds into MIDFL, some into the Borneo Development Corporation (set up to encourage industrial development in that state) and other resources into electricity, housing, and agriculture. The CDC, while a commercial venture, concerns itself with the developmental requirements of the country and with providing limited technical assistance and training in connection with the schemes it helps to finance.

Singapore

The Economic Development Board of Singapore, while an instrument of that state, has been looked on as a prototype for Malaysia. It was established in 1961 as an autonomous body with an initial capital of $40 million. It provides financial assistance through loans or participation in the equity capital of new industries, gives technical advice, and undertakes feasibility studies for prospective investors. It also has broad planning and implementing responsibilities with respect to industrial estates. It administers certain of the ordinances governing benefits to new industries.

India

The financial institutions of India concerned with industrial development are, of course, numerous.[2] The Reserve Bank of India is the central bank, exercising control over the commercial banks. These latter invest largely in government securities and to a modest extent in industrial issues. In recent years commercial banks have increasingly aided industrial development by providing firms with working capital and by the purchase and discount of inland bills. Thus, the short-term needs of Indian industry and trade are reasonably well met.

Since independence a number of special institutions have come into being to meet the rapidly growing requirements of industry for medium- and long-term capital. These include the Industrial Finance Corporation of India, the several state financial corporations, the Refinance Corporation for Industries, the Industrial Credit and Investment Corporation of India, the National Industrial Development Corporation, and the National Small Industries Corporation.

The Industrial Finance Corporation of India was established in 1948 and was the first institution to provide medium— and long-range loans. Its funds are available to public, limited companies and to cooperative societies incorporated in India and engaged in manufacturing, processing, generation and distribution of power, mining, shipping, and hotel operations. It aids both new and established enterprises. It makes loans in either local currency or foreign exchange; guarantees loans; subscribes to stocks or shares; underwrites stocks, shares, bonds or debentures; and guarantees deferred payments for imports and local purchases of capital goods. It can also participate in the equity capital of industrial concerns. Under a 1960 amendment, it can guarantee loans from scheduled or state cooperative banks, and it also can guarantee foreign exchange loans or credits from banks and financial institutions. The Corporation has substantial paid-up capital; its operating funds were raised by issues of bonds and debentures; and it has had foreign exchange loans from the

United States Agency for International Development and other foreign-aid institutions.

The Industrial Credit and Investment Corporation of India, Ltd. (ICICI), is a privately owned institution that was set up primarily to assist private financial investment. Its purposes are to aid in the development, expansion, and modernization of private firms and to encourage private industrial investment, both domestic and foreign. It makes long- and medium-term loans; sponsors and underwrites new issues of shares; guarantees loans from other private investment sources; and furnishes managerial, technical, and administrative advice. The ICICI has capital that is partly paid up and partly subscribed in India, the United Kingdom, and the United States. It also has loans from the Central Government, the World Bank, the United States Agency for International Development, and the Kirdit Anstalt in West Germany.

The State Financial Corporations extend assistance to medium- and small-scale industrial concerns. There are 15 of these corporations.

The Refinance Corporation for Industries assists banking institutions in giving medium-term loans to approved industries in the private sector. Its refinance facilities are available to 57 commercial banks, the 15 state financial corporations, and three state cooperative Banks. Its funds have particularly been channeled into the chemical industry, and the textile, paper, electrical, basic-metals, and cement industries.

The National Industrial Development Corporation was established in 1954 by the government, to pioneer new basic and heavy industries of high priority status under the national industrial development program. It accomplishes its objective through the preparation of projects and blueprints for industrial schemes, and through the establishment of companies to carry them out. It has also provided financial assistance to the jute and cotton textile industries.

The National Small Industries Corporation was established in 1955 to promote small-scale industry. It obtains government orders for such industries and assists them financially and with technical advice. It also works with larger firms to obtain parts and accessories orders for small plants. It arranges for machinery acquisition on a hire-purchase basis. Its funds come from the government of India, in the form of paid-up capital subscribed by the government, and from loans. It has also had a loan from the United States Agency for International Development.

Pakistan

Pakistan, as the result of partition from India, was faced with serious problems with respect to banking facilities. The Reserve Bank of India had functioned as the central bank for the whole Indo-Pakistan subcontinent. The commercial banks had been operated largely by Hindus who, for the most part, left Pakistan after partition. There were no development banks.

In mid-1948 the State Bank of Pakistan was organized as the central bank, with responsibility for maintaining monetary stability, defending the currency, and promoting economic development. It has wide powers of monetary and credit control and is the sole note-issuing authority. It manages the public debt of both the central and provincial governments. It was the sponsor of the National Bank of Pakistan, which provides a nationwide system of banks. It has played a key role in establishing the Institute of Bankers, which is training a professional corps of young bankers to replace those who departed at the time of partition.

Commercial banks in Pakistan have had to go through a major rejuvenation. The progress has been substantial. They are now the most important source of organized credit and play a major role in meeting the credit requirements of commerce and the working capital requirements of industry. To meet industrial needs for long- and medium-term credit, the government, in 1949, set up the Pakistan Industrial Finance Corporation (PIFC). Its scope was limited, however, since it could not finance the establishment of new industries nor could it grant loans against prospective assets. To meet these and other deficiencies, in 1957 the government created the Pakistan Industrial Credit and Investment Corporation (PICIC). Sixty percent of the share capital of PICIC is financed by Pakistani private investors; 40 percent by private shareholders in the United States, the United Kingdom, Canada, Japan, and West Germany. In addition, PICIC receives loans from the central government and lines of credit in foreign currencies from the World Bank, several international aid agencies, and foreign governments. To aid in the development of the capital market, it underwrites shares and also matches entrepreneurial investment.

In 1961, the Industrial Development Bank (IDB) was established as successor to the PIFC. The government has subscribed 51 percent of the share capital; the rest is held by the public. The IDB is principally concerned with providing long-term credits to medium and small industries. It also administers a number of foreign loans on behalf of the government.

Iran

In Iran the government-owned Bank Melli for many years not only engaged in commercial banking operations but also functioned as a central bank by issuing notes and acting as a reserve bank. In 1961 the Central Bank was established, having the functions typical of such organizations. The Bank Melli is now limited to commercial operations but holds about half of the assets and liabilities of the whole commercial banking system.

In 1959 the Industrial and Mining Development Bank of Iran was set up as a private industrial development bank. Iranian investors hold 60 percent of the stock; foreign investors the balance. The bank mobilizes private savings and other domestic financial resources and directs them to industrial, transportation, and mining enterprises. In addition, it is concerned with attracting foreign capital and technical and managerial skills to such enterprises. It has also cooperated with the government in establishing a stock market.

In 1961 the government created the Industrial Guarantee Fund, through the initiative of the Plan Organization and the Ministry of Industry and Mines. The Fund provides loans to small businesses for the acquisition of new machinery.

The Industrial Credit Bank is government owned and was created for the purpose of financing small-scale industrial projects other than those which are government owned. It has financed sugar mills, textile plants, cement factories, vegetable-oil-processing factories, leather and shoe industries, and truck and bus assembly plants. In addition to its financing activities, it conducts economic surveys and feasibility studies.

Turkey

In Turkey institutional arrangements for the allocation of funds for industrial development have been characterized by the Turkish State Planning Organization in these terms:

> The increase of savings in the private sector and allocation of these funds to the most productive fields depend upon the existence of a well-functioning capital market. Unfortunately this is completely lacking in Turkey. Except for public funds, capital is closely tied to its owner. This makes concentration of small capital funds impossible. It is, therefore, mandatory to reorganize institutions like the banking system, social insurance organizations, and stock exchanges in such a way as to create a capital market.[3]

The 1964 annual program of the First Five-Year Development Plan called for establishing institutions to finance industry by issuing or guaranteeing shares or bonds.

In 1963 legislation was enacted to set up the State Investment Bank for the financing of industry in the public sector. To support industrial development in the private sector, five Turkish commercial banks have organized the Industrial Investment and Credit Bank, a medium-term bank using 1 percent of their deposits as the capital fund of the bank, together with loans from U.S.-generated (Public Law 480) funds, and plans were laid for a Mining Development Bank.

Since 1954 Turkey has had a foreign investment law for the purpose of guaranteeing, within limits, the principal and interest of foreign loans to enterprises important to the economic development of the country. Commercial banks have also provided capital. However, much development capital from such sources in recent years has gone into activities not central to the nation's planned growth, e.g., luxury housing.

In 1962 and 1963 a series of seminars were held in Turkey, attended by specialists and high-level officials, to consider the technical problem of capital formation and investment in industry. These seminars, sponsored by the Economic and Social Studies Conference Board, the Turkish Management Association, and the Industrial Development Bank, resulted in a series of recommendations that, if implemented, could go far toward vitalizing the whole industrial development effort of the country.

Israel

Israel's central bank, the Bank of Israel, performs all of the usual functions of such units. There are a number of other financial institutions, including mortgage banks, the Tourist Industry Development Corporation, unit trusts, investment companies, several commercial banking organizations, and the Industrial Bank of Israel (IDBI).

The IDBI was established in 1957, through the initiative of the government of Israel, the country's three largest commercial banks, the Histadrut (the General Federation of Jewish Labor in Israel), and the Manufacturers' Association of Israel. Other local banks and private investors joined later. The Bank's function is to aid new and expanding industry with medium- and long-term loans. The Bank usually charges 8 percent interest but may offer lower rates to enterprises going to areas of the country designated for special development. Principal and interest are linked to the U.S. dollar or to the cost-of-living index. The Bank provides a major portion of net credit advanced to industry.

Loans are made by the IDBI out of its capital funds and funds allocated by the government in the Development Budget. When taken from the latter source, loans are made in accordance with government priorities by type of industry, geographical location of plants, and extent to which production is designated for export. Otherwise, loans may be made without regard to government policy. Increasingly, the IDBI has taken over the financing of Israeli industrial development. Most U.S. aid for industry, as well as other foreign investments, is handled through it.

The IDBI has participated with the government in setting up a subsidiary company, Industrial Development Bank of Israel Investment Company, Ltd., which invests in the share capital of various firms. The Investment Company is not only supplying venture capital but is also participating in the overall management of companies whose shares it has purchased. The Bank, in turn, supplies professional and administrative services for project evaluation, auditing and control, costing, organization and legal problems, construction, marketing, management, and production activities.

The Discount Bank Investment Corporation, Ltd., was established in 1961 to channel private investors' funds into industrial development. The company has a diversified portfolio, participates in the management of the enterprises it invests in, and has begun granting long-term industrial loans, using primarily special deposits of the government of Israel's account.

These varied approaches to mobilizing and disseminating funds for industrial development suggest that in many modernizing nations this is a subject of substantial concern. In addressing this concern, questions of the following type may be useful to pose: What are the capital requirements of the country for industrial development over the next decade? What proportion of these needs will be met out of the government's regular resources from taxation, income from government enterprises, etc.? What proportion will be met out of special governmental resources designated for industrial development? Are significant shifts in the availability of such funds over the next decade anticipated that may suggest the need for new sources and new institutions? Are present savings institutions adequate? Are there substantial savings which might be effected with the creation of new savings institutions, stock markets, investment corporations? Are foreign sources of capital being fully exploited and utilized? Is public education with respect to savings called for? How fully are the relationships between savings, price and wage levels, balance of payments, and national economic development being considered officially and being interpreted to the public? Are present institutional arrangements for meeting long- and medium-term capital requirements adequate? How satisfactory is the market for short-term loans for factory mortgage purposes, purchase of machinery, and operating capital? Are foreign loans and grants that provide equity or working capital being effectively channeled to the most relevant industrial development activities? Are the potentialities for management participation on the part of government or private investment organizations in new industrial enterprises being fully exploited? Are there needs for planning and technical assistance in the development of new enterprises that are not now being met and that can appropriately accompany the capital allocation system? Finally, and probably most important, does the system of capital allocation receive

adequate guidance from government with respect to enterprise
that should receive priority assistance to achieve balanced national
social and economic growth?

Notes

1. Adapted from Malayan Industrial Development Finance, Ltd., *Capital for Industry* (Singapore: Tien Wah Press, Ltd., n.d.), pp. 2-3.

2. Indian Investment Center, *Investing in India... Basic Facts of the Indian Economy* (New Delhi, 1962). Much of the detailed information which follows is derived from this source.

3. Turkey, State Planning Organization, *Introducing Turkey's State Planning Organization* (Ankara: Union of Chambers of Commerce, Industry, and Commodity Exchanges, 1963), p. 19.

6 Inducements to the Private Sector

Almost all of the countries of Asia, Africa, and Latin America that are in the process of social and economic development and that have mixed economies provide advisory services to new and expanding industries, as well as a number of other inducements. The advisory services include feasibility studies, market analyses, technical aid, cost- and quality-control guidance, and training and promotional assistance. The inducements take many forms, of which the most important is a variety of tax benefits. In addition, plant facilities may be provided under favorable financing terms. Roads, power and water supplies, and other essential services may also be supplied. In a number of countries these facilities and services are created in specially designed industrial estates. Particular attention may be given to assisting small industries, because of the need for such enterprises and because the small-scale entrepreneur lacks know-how and wherewithal. In general, the objective in providing advice and inducements is to encourage industrial growth in directions commensurate with development plans and goals.

Advisory Arrangements and Services

The advisory arrangements and services provided by several countries, as well as the patterns of inducements to industry, are considered below. Reference is made to certain related matters, such as the buildup of infrastructure, licensing, materials and foreign-exchange allocation processes, price and wage controls and research as a stimulant to economic development. In a final section, tariff provisions and manpower programs to encourage the private sector's development are discussed.

The Philippines

In the Philippines the central agency with responsibility for advising private investors on government plans and procedures and for coordinating proposed private industrial projects with public projects is the Program Implementation Agency (PIA). The PIA translates national goals, as set by the National Economic Council, into packages of projects and coordinates and sets priorities among them. It also prescribes government incentive policies and seeks to remove administrative bottlenecks to industrial development.

As a means of informing investors about the opportunities available in the Philippines, the Department of Commerce and Industry has published *Guidelines for Foreign Investors in the Philippines*. This succinctly summarizes a number of facts about the Philippines that may be of interest to potential investors on topics such as investment opportunities, the labor force, the agricultural and manufacturing economies, foreign trade, and economic development. *Guidelines* reviews investment guarantees, including the constitutional guarantees of property rights and compensation for expropriated properties. The relatively few import and export and foreign-exchange restrictions are considered. Note is taken of constitutional limitations on the exploitation of natural resources by persons other than Filipinos, and it is pointed out that corporations must be at least 60 percent owned by Filipinos. A review of relevant banking and other statutes is provided. *Guidelines* also discusses the investment incentives made available by the government.

Provisions of the Basic Industries Law, as set forth in *Guidelines*, are as follows:

> Republic Act 3127 which took effect on June 17, 1961, commonly known as the Basic Industries Law, provides incentives for investments

in basic industries. This law exempts any person, partnership, company or corporation who or which is not engaged or shall engage in basic industries from the payment of special import tax, compensating tax, and tariff duties in respect to the importation of machinery, spare parts and equipment as follows:

a) 100 percentum of the taxes due during the period from the date of the approval of the Act to December 31, 1966;

b) 75 percentum of the taxes due during the period from January 1 to December 31, 1967;

c) 50 percentum of the taxes due during the period from January 1 to December 31, 1968 after which such person, partnership, company, or corporation shall be liable in full to all taxes.

The basic industries covered by the law are the following:

a)   basic iron, steel, aluminum industries;
b)   basic chemical industries, antibiotics, fungicides, including cement manufacture and its allied industries and fertilizers;
c)   copper, and alumina smelting and refining;
d)   pulping and/or including the integrated manufacture of paper products;
e)   deep-sea fishing and canning of sea foods and manufacture of fish meals, manufacture of nets and other fishing gear;
f)   refining of gold, silver, and other noble metals;
g)   mining and exploration of base or noble minerals or metals and crude oil or petroleum;
h)   production of agricultural crops;
i)   shipbuilding and dry-docking;
j)   coal and dead-burnt dolomite;
k)   cattle industries;
l)   logging and manufacture of veneer and plywood;
m)   vegetable oil manufacturing, processing or refining and manufacture;
n)   irrigational equipment, farm machineries, spare parts and tools for such farm machineries, trucks and automobiles;
o)   production and manufacture of textile, cotton, ramie, synthetic fibers and coconut coir;
p)   manufacture of cigars from both native and Virginia tobacco;
q)   manufacture of gasoline and diesel engines;
r)   manufacture of ceramics, furnaces, refractors and glasses;
s)   manufacture of food products out of cereals, forest and/or agricultural crops.[1]

As an additional incentive, the government introduced in the mid-1960's the Investment Incentives Law, for the purpose of (a) attracting foreign investment capital into the Philippines; and (b) channeling domestic and foreign investments into economic activities which are basic to national development. This law provides that investors in basic industries receive accelerated deductions for both organizational and preoperating expenses and depreciation allowances; carry-over privileges; tax exemptions for importation of machinery and equipment; and eased provisions in the employment of foreign labor. The law also provides special benefits for joint ventures using Philippine and foreign capital when investment is in basic industries.

Guidelines also describes the various business laws governing partnerships, domestic operations, foreign corporations, banks and banking institutions, patents, trademarks, etc. The tax laws, direct (individual and corporate) and indirect; tariffs and customs; and labor laws, including wages and hours, employment of women and children, employee benefits, etc., are all described. Thus, the investor is provided with a complete manual on the benefits and obligations he may encounter when investing in the Philippines.

In the cottage- and small-scale industry field, the Philippines set up in 1962 the National Cottage Industries Development Authority (NACIDA) for the purpose of creating an integrated program of financial, marketing, and technical assistance. In the first two years of its existence, NACIDA processed over 18,000 applications for registration as cottage industries eligible for financial, marketing, and technical assistance and granted about 12,000 registration certificates. About 3,000 of these were granted development loans. Handicraft articles are evaluated from the viewpoint of consumer preferences in design and materials, and the results are disseminated to cottage producers. Further, work has been done on adjusting production techniques to market requirements. Display centers and common service facilities are being set up all over the Philippines. Ten regional institutes provide training in cottage-industry skills. Twenty-three cottage-industry cooperatives have been established to handle the marketing of the goods produced. The success of these products in international trade fairs has led to optimistic judgments on the value of the cottage industries as earners of foreign exchange.

Malaysia

Malaysia's numerous provisions for encouraging industrial development are being developed from the measures that obtained in its individual states.* Pioneer Industries Ordinance No. 31 of Malaya was passed in 1958, providing for income tax exemption for from two to five years, depending on the amount of capital invested in fixed assets. Pioneer industries are defined as ones that, at the time of application for pioneer industry status, are not being carried on in the Federation on a commercial scale. They must be industries with favorable development prospects and ones that, if established, will serve the public interest. Singapore and the Borneo States have similar legislation. By 1970, well over a hundred companies in Malaysia had been granted pioneer status. The Pioneer Industries Law is administered by the Industrial Development Division of the Ministry of Commerce and Industry.

As a complement to this law, the government permits free remittance of capital within the sterling area. Nominal control of capital remittance outside the sterling area is exercised by the Controller of Foreign Exchange. The government also guarantees foreign investments and has concluded investment guarantee agreements with West Germany and the United States. It has a double-taxation accord with the United Kingdom.

MIDFL assists industrialists by lending them part of the cost of both land and factory for the establishment of new plants. Standard factories have been designed and are available to new entrepreneurs in a variety of sizes and styles.

Several industrial estates have been set up, such as those at Kuala Lumpur and Singapore, which provide industrialists with sites at low cost. They come equipped with access roads, water, sewerage, and electric power. Through the estates, industries obtain immediate land title, something that is frequently difficult to accomplish under Asian land-tenure systems. The federal government of Malaysia has set up trust funds to permit its state governments to develop such estates, since they provide for orderly industrial development close to population centers.

The National Productivity Center was created in Kuala Lumpur in 1961, with International Labor Organisation assistance, for the

---

*In this discussion references are made to Singapore, which is presently independent but was formerly a state of Malaysia and as such contributed its experience to the formulation of national policies for Malaysia.

purposes of increasing productivity and training managers for industry. The Ministry of Labor and the Ministry of Education are both placing much emphasis on providing technical training for industry, particularly through apprenticeship training schemes. In Singapore the Economic Development Board conducts feasibility studies and provides technical assistance to industry though the Small Industries Service Unit and the Industrial Research Unit.

The Malaysians have been alert to the importance of publicizing the opportunities and assistance available for new and expanding industry. MIDFL has issued publications informing the public, such as *Capital for Industry* and *Factory Mortgage Finance.* The Ministry of Commerce and Industry has issued numerous information sheets, including one entitled *Facilities for Industrial Development,* which states:

> If you invest in industry in the Federation, you can take advantage of the many facilities provided by the Government;
>
> RELIEF FROM INCOME TAX for 2-5 years to industries heretofore not carried on in the Federation.
> FREE TRANSFER OF CAPITAL AND EARNINGS within the Sterling Area and with minimum of control to area outside the Sterling Area.
> PROTECTION OF FOREIGN INVESTMENTS against expropriation.
> TARIFF PROTECTION to deserving local industries.
> IMPORT DUTY EXEMPTION for machinery and in some cases for raw materials for industrial development.
> PROTECTION AGAINST DUMPING by foreign exporters.
> INDUSTRIAL ESTATES providing cheap and readily available serviced sites.
> DEVELOPMENT OF BASIC SERVICES TO INDUSTRY such as roads, ports, power and communication facilities.
> LOAN FACILITIES FOR INDUSTRY through the Malayan Industrial Development Finance Limited.
> PRODUCTIVITY TRAINING for management and supervisory personnel in local industry.
> INDUSTRIAL RESEARCH FACILITIES through the proposed Department of Scientific and Industrial Research.[2]

The program of assistance to industry in Malaysia is impressive. Relationships of specific industrial developments to the planned goals for the economy are still evolving. Singapore has detailed lists of industries and products, accompanied by economic and technical feasibility studies, which are prepared by its Economic Development Board. Lying ahead is the task of setting priorities, as the result of broad economic studies and interindustry analyses, and the preparation of integrated plans that coordinate tariff policy, internal markets, and other elements of the development program.

India

Indian practice with respect to advice and inducements to the private industrial sector is interesting, since economically India is dependent on private enterprise for the vast bulk of its national income, yet ideologically it embraces socialism and detailed planning.

The Indian Investment Center was established in 1961 "to encourage Indian and foreign entrepreneurs in exploring the possibilities of setting up new industrial undertakings in the country, and to assist them in pooling their resources for implementing sound and viable projects on a joint venture basis."[3] The Center has issued a number of publications on the Indian economy, on its own operations, and on the rules, regulations and procedures governing private investment activity. It has set up branch offices in New York and other foreign cities.

The principal functions of the Investment Center are, in its own words:

> To promote wider knowledge and understanding, in the capital-exporting centres of the world, of conditions, laws, policies and procedures pertaining to investment in India and of investment opportunities in India;
> To advise and assist Indian industrialists, including those engaged in medium and small industries, on matters necessary to attract foreign private capital and/or techniques;
> To advise and assist foreign businessmen on matters pertaining to investment in India; and for this purpose, if necessary, to establish branch offices abroad;
> To undertake surveys of foreign investment possibilities and studies in relation to particular industries;
> To undertake by the diffusion of knowledge and information, implementation of programmes designed to encourage and promote the flow of private capital into India in a manner most helpful to the Indian economy and the Indian Five Year Plans.[4]

Before a new enterprise can be established, approval of location, capacity, and other details must be obtained. Approval is granted through issuance of a license, required by the Industries Act of 1951. A license is needed for the import of capital equipment and machinery. The terms of foreign collaboration, if there is to be any, must also be approved. The issuance of capital is controlled by the Capital Issues Act of 1947, and registration of the enterprise as a corporate concern by the Companies Act of 1956.

The criteria for licensing under the Industries Act are that the product to be manufactured is important to the national economy; that the proposal is in accord with capacity targets and prior commitments under the Third Five-Year Plan; that the enterprise will contribute to balanced regional development; and that satisfactory terms of investment or collaboration have been arrived at where foreign capital is involved.

Under the Third Five-Year Plan the criteria for approving enterprises were spelled out in a schedule of priorities and conditions that illustrates the extent to which the Indian government guides industrial development in planned directions. Priority was given to schemes already initiated under the Second Five-Year Plan or deferred from that plan because of foreign-exchange limits; to industries whose present capacity is underutilized; to heavy engineering and machine building industries; to fertilizer manufacturers; to producers of aluminum, mineral oils, and basic organic and inorganic chemicals; and to manufacturers of essential goods such as drugs, paper, cloth, sugar, vegetable oils and housing materials. In addition, balanced regional growth was to be furthered through evaluation of locational plans and encouragement of village industry. Special encouragement was given to projects oriented toward export promotion.

Many sources of advice and technical assistance are available to the investor in India. Illustrative are reports of the Indian Statistical Institute's Planning Unit (done in cooperation with the Massachusetts Institute of Technology) on the structure of the Indian economy. These deal, for example, with plant size, location, and time-phasing for selected industries.

Redesigning Indian manufactured products to fit the needs of foreign buyers has been a concern of the Indian Co-operative Union of New Delhi. Styling and merchandising experts from

Europe and the United States have been brought in to study the craft and handloom products of traditional village industries and suggest design and product innovations that would appeal to Western buyers. The Union also provided training for Co-operative members to assist in the production of marketable goods.

A number of tax incentives to encourage industrial development are offered by the Indian government. These include the following:

1. Tax holidays are granted to new industrial enterprises for a period of up to five years. Taxes are forgiven on profits of up to 6 percent on the capital employed. Dividends paid out of the exempted profits are also exempt from taxes.

2. In addition to liberal depreciation allowances, a development rebate equal to 20 percent of the cost of plant and machinery is allowed as a deduction from the taxable income in the year of installation.

3. Dividends received by either an Indian or foreign company engaged in specified industries are exempt from supertax, i.e., they are taxed at the rate of 25 percent.

4. Dividends from Indian companies that are not entitled to supertax exemptions are given the benefit of low tax rates.

A variety of other tax benefits are available, including tax-free loans; carry-forward of losses and allowances; deductions for expenditures for scientific research, royalties, and technical personnel; regates on export earnings; etc.

The 1964-65 budget of the government of India offered a number of adjustments in the tax rate designed to make foreign investment more profitable. Policy with respect to foreign exchange has encouraged the inflow of foreign currencies for industrial activity in line with planned objectives. It has also permitted expatriating investments and income earned, under specified conditions.

An investment-guarantee agreement has been worked out with the United States. Private U.S. investors, for a small premium, can obtain a guarantee from the U.S. government for the reconvertibility into U.S. dollars of the proceeds from the sale of their investments in India. Payments to U.S. investors in the event of expropriation is also covered.

During the period of the Second Five-Year Plan, about 60 industrial estates were set up, primarily to provide factory facilities. For the most part they were located near or in large cities and had a tendency to reinforce population and production concentrations. Under the Third Plan it is anticipated that about 300 additional industrial estates will be established, with emphasis this time on location in or near small and medium-sized towns. Also, it was planned to build a number of rural estates in areas where power, water supply, and other facilities are available or could be readily provided. A rural industrial estate consists mainly of worksheds for use by artisans, together with certain common services and facilities. Care is being taken to locate such estates in areas where there is a sufficient concentration of artisans and craftsmen to use improved techniques and tools and modern facilities.

Considerable emphasis has been placed on the development of small industries in India.[5] An elaborate organization exists in the central government to provide technical and advisory services to small industries. The Central Small Industries Organization (CSIO) has several coordinating divisions, 17 state and four branch small industries service institutes, and about 60 specialized extension and training centers. The CSIO has several hundred technical staff members and shop employees, as well as numerous administrative and service personnel.

Services performed by the CSIO and its various units include technical advice and instruction to small industrial units on improved technical processes and on the use of modern machinery and equipment; preparation of designs and drawings for machines and machine parts, equipment, etc., since small industrialists do not ordinarily have the know-how for machine design; technical help in the use of raw materials, plant layout, selection of machinery and equipment, and quality control; demonstrations of technical processes, especially on industrial estates where well-equipped workshops for demonstration purposes may be found; conduct of training programs in such subjects as blueprint reading and heat treatment and foundry, either in institute classes or in-plant training; technical assistance to small units to aid in serving effectively as ancillary producers or subcontractors to larger industrial units; guidance in business management, including marketing, financial and cost accounting, production management, industrial engineering, factory legislation, personnel relations, etc.; conduct of economic surveys in particular industries and geographic areas, with proposals for specific development activities (as part of this effort an economic information service is provided for small industrialists, together with industry outlook reports and other types of factual or advisory economic reporting).

In addition to these central government efforts on behalf of small industry, a number of agencies of state governments concern themselves with the development of small-scale industry, including state directorates of industries, state small industries corporations, state financial corporations, and state directorates of economics and industrial statistics. The directorates of industries provide credit, power, land for workshops, allocation of controlled raw materials, issuance of certificates of essentiality, and training and demonstration assistance. At the district level, district industry offices aid the development of small industries and also encourage handicrafts and village industries.

The importance of infrastructure for industrial purposes has been recognized since the time of the First Five-Year Plan. *Investing in India* contains a report on the infrastructure situation covering power, coal, transport and communications, railways, roads, shipping, ports, air transport, communications (post offices and telephones), and social services (education, medical facilities, manpower, wages, and community development).[6]

Pakistan

Pakistan, concerned with developing a favorable climate for private investment, established the Investment Promotion Bureau in 1961 to serve as a clearing house for investors. The Bureau disseminates information on investment opportunities and conditions and assists in obtaining import licenses, land, and building materials. It provides or will secure technical advice for the investor and negotiate on his behalf with the central or provincial government. As an aid to the production of goods that meet acceptable standards of quality, the Pakistan Standards Institution is preparing and publishing sets of national standards.

Under Pakistan's Second Five-Year Plan the government put considerable emphasis on strengthening vocational schools and on the promotion of technical training in industry. The Council of Scientific and Industrial Research concerns itself with research on the nature and use of raw-material resources and the development of new products. The results of the Council's investigations are made available to industry for commercial exploitation.

In the preparation of economically and technologically sound projects, considerable use has been made of foreign experts. A firm of industrial consultants has carried out a detailed survey of industrial development possibilities in East Pakistan. In West Pakistan, with assistance from the United Nations Special Fund and private consultants, the opportunities for an integrated steel complex have been studied. The Industrial Research and Development Center of East Pakistan is also engaging in this type of survey. The Pakistan Industrial Technical Assistance Centers in Karachi and Lahore have studied problems of industrial productivity and have examined issues related to sound preparation of projects.

A number of tax incentives are provided by the Pakistani government to encourage industrial growth. Enterprises begun during the Second Plan were generally exempt from taxation for four, six, or eight years, depending on their geographic location. There are liberal depreciation allowances, and losses may be carried forward for six years. No restrictions exist on the remission of profits and on the repatriation of capital in approved industries. Agreements have been reached with a number of countries on the avoidance of double taxation. Foreign technicians working in approved industries are exempt from income taxes for a two-year period.

During the Second Plan the trend in Pakistan was strongly in the direction of freeing the entrepreneur from governmental restrictions and of increasing reliance on market forces. Some critics of Pakistani tax and other fiscal policies feel much more must be done to encourage capital retention for reinvestment purposes. Nevertheless, the performance of the private sector has been strong, suggesting that the policies of disengagement from extensive government control are successful.

Iran

The Iranian program of advice and inducements to aid private sector industrial development was projected in *Outline of the Third Plan*.[7] The main objective under the Third Plan was "to develop and expand those industries which will contribute to a maximum increase in national income." Beyond its capital credit measures, the government is instituting favorable tax and tariff policies. It also is subsidizing surveys for the establishment of new industries and encouraging an influx of foreign skills.

The Plan outline noted that the tax structure could be modified to increase savings and to channel investment toward desired industries. More liberal depreciation allowances were proposed to provide incentives for reinvestment and expansion. Undistributed profits, when used for reinvestment, were to be tax exempt. Capital-goods imports, now exempt from customs duties, were to remain so, and imports of raw materials were to be taxed at lower rates. Tax holidays for five years to new industries approved by the Ministry of Commerce were to be continued. As an inducement to entrepreneurs to locate in areas particularly needing development, the Plan outline proposed tax holidays of longer duration. It also proposed that tariffs and commercial benefit taxes on raw materials used for the production of goods sold to the oil companies should be eliminated, since the oil companies are exempt from import taxes. Protective tariffs were to be set at a level to encourage home manufacturers.

A characteristic deterrent in Iran to industrial and mining development, in addition to the shortage of capital and skilled manpower, is the lack of carefully prepared surveys and feasibility studies. Because of the high cost of such investigations, the government plans to subsidize their preparation. Some surveys and feasibility studies are made by the Industrial Credit Bank. The Central Bank provides guidelines to potential entrepreneurs on projects and prospects, maintaining a Foreign Investment Center for this purpose.

To encourage medium- and small-scale industry, the government planned to provide banks with special incentives to develop credit services. It proposed to set up three industrial estates and was receiving assistance from the United Nations for this purpose. A survey of small industries in a number of different areas of the country was also planned for the 1964-68 period. Since the most important cottage industry is carpet weaving, the government anticipated expanding the Iran Carpet Company to engage in the promotion of exports and in product development.

Recognizing that infrastructure is essential to industrial development, the Third Plan outline proposed to develop road, railway, airport, port, and postal and telecommunications systems. Progress having been made on a national highway network, attention was directed to feeder roads to connect villages and underdeveloped resource areas with the highway network. The Iranian State Railway is being extended to the Turkish border, and additional rolling stock is being provided. The long-range airport development program envisions adequate facilities for international carriers, an improved system of airports for domestic carriers, and the integration of civil and military air requirements. Construction of the port of Bandar Abbas and of small coastal-vessel ports along the Persian Gulf were projected for the latter part of the Third Plan period, in order to offer development opportunities for the southeast region.

Turkey

Turkish experience with respect to providing advice and incentives to encourage private industrial development appears to reflect the somewhat ambiguous state of mind that has long prevailed on the merits of private versus state enterprise. The government has not played a vigorous advisory role, nor has it enacted much legislation designed to stimulate private investment. On the other hand, it has indirectly encouraged the private sector, and many leading citizens and public servants are hopeful that in the future more will be done directly by the government to stimulate the private economy.

The Union of Chambers of Commerce, Industry, and Commodity Exchanges, a quasi-private organization that was created by law, maintains the Turkish Investment Promotion and Information Center. The purposes of this Center are several: to provide the entrepreneur with information on tax legislation, laws and regulations governing employer-employee relationships, banking and financial practices, and corporate regulations; to develop summaries of the present state of specific industries, market projections, data on raw materials sources and supplies, labor information, and water, power, and other infrastructure data; to prepare information for foreign consumption on desirable investment opportunities; to undertake, at the request of prospective investors, market research, economic analyses, and preinvestment surveys; and to serve as a point of contact with public and private investment banks, financial institutions, and development agencies. The Union also has a unit, the Department of Industry, whose function is to undertake studies and surveys on behalf of private investors; to make recommendations on the important export of industrial raw materials, semiprocessed and finished goods; to conduct studies related to demand, capacity, quality, standardization, and cost; to advise on industrial development of backward areas; and to serve as liaison to the State Planning Organization on matters related to industrialization. An additional function of the Union has been the allocation of government import licenses to private sector importers.

As of the mid-1960's, the government had no provisions for tax forgiveness as such but was considering the development of a program and had identified those branches of industry that may receive special tax treatment on undistributed profits. In 1963 a system of accelerated depreciation was inaugurated to encourage investment in technological improvements. Foreign investors are afforded certain guarantees and benefits under the Foreign Investment Encouragement Law, the most important provisions of which relate to the repatriation of profits and capital of foreign investors under specified conditions and to the equal treatment of foreign and domestic capital.

In recent years a good many measures have been under consideration in Turkey designed to aid or stimulate industry to grow in directions considered desirable from the overall national-development viewpoint. Reductions in import duties on capital goods have been contemplated. A committee of the Ministry of Industry sought to foster the use of Turkish materials in new industries. An increased tax is to be levied on investment

in luxury housing as a means of redirecting capital into more
socially useful channels. A committee of government ministers
studied the possibility of setting up industrial parks. Small
handicraft industries are being encouraged.

The Union of Chambers of Commerce, Industry, and
Commodity Exchanges has encouraged potential investors to
move into enterprises of relevance to the Plan and has proposed
to the government measures to encourage investment in line with
the Plan, such as the selective use of customs; encouragement of
private savings; formation of publicly owned (as contrasted with
state-owned) companies; and the development of a pattern of
incentives that would include tax exemptions, depreciation
allowances, import-duty exemptions, tax credits for training
programs, and improved credit resources.

Israel

In Israel, while the governmental role is important to the whole
developmental process, there is a strong emphasis on
macroeconomic planning and declining use of detailed plans and
specific controls. In commenting on the results of the 1960-65
forecast with respect to industrial development, the Israeli
Minister of Finance and of Trade and Industry wrote:

> If you ask which of the two played a greater role in attaining the
> targets of this forecast (1960-65)—accurate planning or the inherent
> capacity of the economy—I would accord preference to Israel's
> economic powers and resources. The foundations of our industry are
> so strong and so solid that even planning a job which was incomplete,
> could be realized.[8]

Thus, Israel has a relatively modest set of advisory services and
inducements to industry, because the inherent strength of the
economy has resulted in voluntary expansion at a rate unequaled
by most other countries, developing or otherwise.

The Ministry of Trade and Industry is the source of much of
the assistance and advice proffered to industry. Its Planning
Division has engaged in preparing specific industrial projects for
the consideration of foreign investors. Before 1962 this was the
principal work of the Division, and it annually prepared about 30
projects. These were then used by the Investment Service to

attract foreign entrepreneurs. Since 1962 the Division has engaged in planning more broadly, producing the *Programme for Israel's Industrial Development, Second Outline, 1965-1970.* The *Programme*, while not dealing with certain matters such as locational issues and alternative strategies, is an important source of information to the industrial community of Israel, as well as to potential investors.

The *Programme* outlined the services being offered to industry as follows:

> Increasing attention is being focused on the improvement and perfection of existing industrial services. Much of the Ministry's time is devoted to drawing up standards and labeling regulations. The training of executives in all branches of management; training and research institutes; collaboration between manufacturers; improved use of materials; better production procedures and quality control; standardization of production—these are all receiving a growing share of the Ministry's time and concern. Manpower problems are playing an ever increasing role both in thought and action in the development of vocational schools, secondary and higher professional education, in-plant training, modern methods for the advancement of workers.[9]

A number of other organizations concern themselves with advisory and analytical assistance designed to encourage industrial development, including the Industrial Council of the Ministry of Trade and Industry, the Investment Center, the Standards Institute, the Israel Company of Fairs and Exhibitions, the Israel Export Institute, the Joint Council for Industrial Productivity and Predirection, and the Central Bureau of Statistics.

The development of infrastructures has been a major concern of the government. It is pursuing the buildup of a national road network, as well as the improvement of harbors and the supplies of water and electricity throughout the country. It has established industrial plants and industrial sites for the use of individual entrepreneurs. In pursuing these activities, the government has been eager to encourage, through tax policies and other means, the dispersal of industries to priority regions in need of special developmental assistance.

The inducements offered to achieve industrial dispersal are stated in the *Programme* as follows:

The grant of loans from the Development Budget;

Approval of projects and Government loans under the Law for the Encouragement of Capital Investments without demanding the securities and commitments required to qualify for this assistance in the rest of the country;

Government participation in the preliminary planning of the plants and provision of basic facilities and services, such as access road, preparation of land and drainage, supply of electricity, water and sewage, and technical, economic and administrative aid and instruction, as well as other preferential conditions;

Financial assistance for the vocational training of an adequate team of workers, in cooperation with the Ministry of Labor;

Allocation of land at convenient prices;

Direction of professional and skilled personnel among the new immigrants to the new plants, in cooperation with the Absorption Department of the Jewish Agency and the Ministry of the Interior.

Protective Tariffs

Governments of the modernizing countries have adopted a variety of other measures for the purpose of aiding and stimulating private industrial development. Among the more important of these are protective tariffs to permit new and expanding industries to establish themselves without the threat of foreign competition.

The use of tariffs to protect infant industries, long a classic policy of industrializing nations, is not the simple matter that it was in the era before the advent of common markets, the widespread, nearly universal efforts to industrialize, the complex functioning of the international money markets, with attendant delicate balance of trade problems, and other factors, such as efficiency of potential industries and administrative capacity to handle regulatory activities.

The Philippines

Tariff policy in the Philippines serves not only as a means of protecting infant industries but also as a means of raising revenue for the government and as an instrument for bargaining with other governments while negotiating trade relationships. The Philippine Tariff and Customs Code is based on the Brussels nomenclature. It contains a list of banned goods, such as narcotics, and a list of exempted items used for scientific, educational, medical and religious purposes. Protective rates of duty are imposed on goods that are produced locally in adequate supply to meet demand. These rates have characteristically been high, but under the policies of recent governments, which emphasize decontrol, they are likely to decline. In addition, if progress is made in the establishment of a common market among the Philippines, Indonesia, and Malaysia, there will be further impetus to reduce protective tariffs. With the rapid spread of industrialization, a decline in protection will in all probability increase the average efficiency of domestic producers.

Malaysia

Malaysian policy with respect to tariffs is particularly complex, because the member states have differing interests at stake in their tariff policies; the development of a Malaysian Common Market[10] would bring into sharp focus these differences. The practices followed by the government of Malaya with respect to tariffs and protection to "pioneer" industries are illustrative of how national policy for Malaysia may evolve.

The Tariff Advisory Committee (subsequently superseded by the Tariff Advisory Board with membership from the Malaysian states) was created within Malaya's Ministry of Commerce and Industry to review and advise on all tariff policy. The position of the government with respect to tariff protection was set forth by the Ministry:

> The Government has agreed that assistance by way of exemption or partial exemption from import duties on materials imported for manufacturing purposes, and a moderate measure of tariff protection should be accorded to local industry. Such exemption and protection will be given where it is proved to the satisfaction of the Government that it is necessary and will not be abused, and that the undertaking concerned is operating. . .in an efficient manner. The margin of protection granted will obtain for the local manufacturers the market for goods which can be economically produced in the Federation within a reasonable period. In considering an application for exemption or protection the Government will also bear constantly in mind the interests of the consumer and the effect of tariff changes on the public revenue and the balance of payments position of the Federation. The Government will not grant exemption or protection to an extent which would permit the marketing of goods of inferior quality or at excessive prices in comparison with imported goods. It will not grant tariff concessions to industry to an extent which would materially affect public revenue. [11]

Singapore

Singapore, which is as interested in industrialization as Malaysia, faces the problem of retaining and sustaining its very important entrepot role and at the same time building up its industries. The prospect of accomplishing this remains unclear, since it is evident that the use of more than a very modest system of protection through tariffs could pose problems for Singapore's trade interests.

India

Because of India's severe balance of payments problem, a stringent licensing system for imports has been in operation for many years. In general, Indian import policy is designed to serve purposes beyond merely keeping the drain on foreign currency reserves under control—purposes such as assuring that imports are devoted to national-development priorities and that they do not compete with domestically produced products. The Indian Investment Center states that the opportunities are substantial for taking advantage of the larger domestic market under favorable "sheltered" conditions because of the government's policy of protection of home industries.[12]

An interesting cautionary note on this policy is quoted because of its general relevance to the modernizing countries, which widely use protection of domestic enterprises as an inducement to investment:

> It is the nature of an import displacing development strategy, of the sort India has adopted, to create by means of import restrictions a quasi-monopolistic, hot-house environment for the protected indigenous industries. Such an environment probably is essential for getting the local industrial growth to take root. But it is also precisely the environment most likely to nurture inattention to production costs, slack scheduling and controls, inefficient, unimaginative marketing, and general managerial slovenliness in the new enterprises. To the extent that the environment is allowed to work these effects, it tends to weaken domestic industry's chance for survival should it ever be re-exposed to the rigors of foreign competition, and, even more surely, it dangerously limits the economy's development of an effective ability to export.
>
> One of the most critical, if less conspicuous, of India's industrialization problems, therefore, is to contrive effective substitutes for international competition as a stimulator of operational efficiency

in the newer industrial enterprises. Although government regulation may not be an entirely fruitless avenue to explore in this regard, compulsory controls generally are very clumsy instruments for inducing efficiency. Much of the answer probably lies in the development of a professional managerial class that accords operational efficiency a high place among its professional standards. Another part can be supplied by making Indian industrialists much more broadly export-minded and by creating inducements to export which do not, at the same time, exempt exporters from meeting the rigors of foreign competition. Another part of the substitute for international competition may be provided by the promotion of domestic competition—both among public, private and mixed enterprises and within markets supplied entirely by private producers.[13]

Pakistan

Pakistan has followed the practice of offering protection from foreign competition as an inducement to investors. It also has engaged in stringent licensing of imports. Pakistan has tended in general, in recent years, to rely more heavily on market forces and less on direct controls than has India. Thus, a policy of protection may require less special action to assure operational efficiency than might otherwise be the case.

Iran and Turkey

Iran and Turkey both offer protection to domestic industries by restricting competitive imports. Iran's *Outline of the Third Plan* notes that in the future such import restrictions must be handled in a manner to avoid undue costs to the Iranian consumer.

Israel

In Israel the policy of the government is now moving in the direction of exposing domestic industries to foreign competition. Until recently, however, an active inducement to investment in Israel was the protection afforded against such competition. Under the protectionist policy hundreds of new industries came into being. But many of these were officially characterized by "inefficiency, low quality, lack of initiative in developing new types and designs, and in industrial research, and investments—which in the long run proved unprofitable to the economy as a whole."[14] It is hoped that through exposure to foreign imports these weaknesses will disappear. It is expected that with the elimination of inferior quality goods, those which are poorly packaged or designed, etc., domestic industries can concentrate on more attractive commodities.

Training of Manpower

A classic attraction for entrepreneurs in considering the initiation or expansion of industrial enterprises is the availability of a substantial and inexpensive supply of labor. Increasingly, governments are recognizing that the abundance of labor alone is not a sufficient inducement to industrialization and that assistance in developing trained manpower for industry is an essential responsibility they must assume. Measures taken by some governments to provide manpower training for industry are discussed below.

The Philippines

The Philippines, among the developing countries, has an unusually high proportion of professionally and technically trained personnel. The University of the Philippines, with a student body of 19,000 and 32 degree-granting units, is the principal source of educated manpower. The great majority of students are trained in agriculture, but the university also prepares business managers and economists for both business and government, as well as civil, mechanical, and electrical engineers and other kinds of professionals. The Labor Education Center prepares personnel for labor-management work. An institute to train extension workers and consultants to assist small industries is under consideration, with emphasis being given to preparation in industrial management, industrial processes and operations, and industrial project development. The Five-Year Integrated Socio-Economic Program calls for the training of at least 300 teachers-technicians yearly, to develop standardization of marketable crafts produced in home industries.

Malaysia

In the 1955 report on the Economic Development of Malaya of the International Bank for Reconstruction and Development

(IBRD),[15] it was noted that only very limited facilities for technical and vocational education were available in Malaya. Four junior technical schools and a technifactory providing preapprentice training were located in the Federation. A technical junior college in Kuala Lumpur offered training to apprentices for the government and for industry. The report recommended the expansion of technical training facilities to produce skilled workers.

The 1961-65 Second Five-Year Plan for Malaya called for a reorganization of the junior technical schools and the addition of a secondary trade school to serve the east coast of the country, the objective being to advance education in vocational crafts and industrial skills. The expansion of the technical college at Kuala Lumpur was also called for, to increase the number of persons receiving advanced technical and engineering education. The National Productivity Center, aided by the U.N. Special Fund, the ILO, and the federal government of Malaya, is already training management in industry in such subjects as layouts for materials handling, production planning and control, cost accounting, and personnel management.

Singapore

Singapore's first development plan, for 1961-64, called for the establishment of 22 vocational/commercial schools, of which two had been opened by the beginning of 1964. A limited amount of training is carried on by the various development corporations. One of the most significant training efforts is made by the Commonwealth Development Corporation, all of whose enterprises concern themselves with on-the-job training of residents of Malaysia and Singapore. The Corporation also sends trainees to London for schooling.

India

India probably had at the time of independence a better supply of skilled personnel available for employment in industrial enterprises than most developing nations. However, with relatively rapid industrialization, demand soon exceeded supply, and it continues to do so. A reading of the training plans for industrial personnel in the Third Five-Year Plan suggests that these are set within a well-developed manpower-planning context. But Lewis has observed that India is still badly in need of much more detailed, *comprehensive* planning of its total phased requirements for, and supplies of, skilled personnel, as well as a comprehensive training program for improving the supply.[16] In spite of this limitation, the provisions of the Third Plan for training personnel required by industry are impressive and indicate the government's strong concern. The capacity of engineering colleges was to be increased by about one-third; that of polytechnical schools by about 50 percent. It was estimated that the requirements for craftsmen will be about 1.3 million during the Plan period. Since numerous industries have their own training programs and a substantial number of workers are trained in the traditional manner of passing on skills from father to son, the total requirement does not have to be met through formal institutional training. Between 1955 and 1961 the number of industrial-training institutes tripled to about 170, and the Third Plan provided for an additional 151.

Apprenticeship training under the Third Plan was to become compulsory, as the voluntary program operative during the Second Plan had not been particularly effective. The major industrial enterprises have set up their own training schools, and some have apprenticeship training programs.

Pakistan

Pakistan suffered the loss through emigration to India of a substantial part of its educated and skilled population. It therefore became imperative that the government exert considerable initiative on the whole education front. The Second Five-Year Plan took cognizance of the special reference to the needs of private enterprise:

> The Government, in association with private enterprise and talent, will need to continue the provision of technical training, scientific and industrial research, services of expert consultants, and collection and compilation of statistics.[17]

The Plan then proposed the strengthening of vocational schools and the promotion of technical training within industrial units, private as well as public. Existing technical training institutions were to be improved and new ones created. Specifically, two agricultural and two technical universitites are being established; the existing engineering colleges are being expanded and two new ones set up, so that the output of engineers will be increased by 75 percent over the Plan period. The polytechnics and technical institutes are also being expanded, and four new polytechnics have been created. This effort, it was estimated, would produce about 1,800 diploma and trained technicians and 6,700 middle-grade technicians annually. In addition, almost all of the semiautonomous organizations (e.g., public corporations and industrial enterprises) conduct internal technical-training programs.

Iran

The Iranian Third Plan *Outline* discussed the industrial manpower situation in the light of the prevailing oversupply of unskilled, untrained workers and the impossibility of absorbing the excess in agriculture. Prevocational training was to be offered on an experimental basis in some primary schools. The Ministry of Labor and the Ministry of Education were to develop programs of vocational training and apprentice and "vestibule" training for new workers. The Ministry of Labor planned to conduct supervisory-training and skill-improvement programs on a large scale, in cooperation with both public and private industries. But the *Outline* noted:

> ... government responsibility for on-the-job training in private plants will be regarded as an emergency measure only. Employers should be expected to assume such responsibility. The government's long-run role in on-the-job training should be limited to the establishment and enforcement of training standards. [18]

The vocational school system in Iran has abandoned its efforts to train craftsmen and foremen and instead is preparing students for industrial employment through intensive courses followed by supervised apprenticeships in industry. These schools are also preparing technicians and offer night courses for adults. It was anticipated that 25,000 graduates would come out of the vocational schools during the Plan period. Ten vocational schools for girls are being added.

While engineers of certain types were still expected to be in moderate surplus at the end of the Plan period, there is a persistent shortage of supporting technicians. The Teheran Polytechnical Institute is training in several critical specialties. One new junior college and two universities with two-year programs in the engineering faculties will also offer training for technologists.

The Plan anticipated an expansion of the government's employment service to provide better analysis of migration patterns and improved labor-market data. The Manpower Coordination Committee is to determine the causes and extent of surplus labor in industry and propose needed legislation and programs to redeploy such surpluses. The Ministry of Education is to take steps to improve the vocational school system, set standards for buildings and equipment, and provide facilities for released-time training of industrial workers. The Armed Forces Vocational Training Program is being launched, which while primarily oriented to rural needs, will also ultimately provide manpower for some types of industrial employment.

Turkey

In Turkey's First Five-Year Development Plan, 1963-1967, it was observed that large numbers of technical personnel and skilled workers were needed to meet the plan's development goals. Since cost and time factors preclude training in schools at present, a program of training within industry was proposed. This is being carried out through vocational-training centers. It is anticipated that more than 3,000 persons will be trained annually in this way.

The plan proposed that in addition to the vocational training centers designed to train foremen, in-service courses be opened in suitable places in each branch of industry. It also pointed out that state economic enterprises, so important in Turkey, are well organized for the training of numerous personnel and that courses offered through this means should be carried out in cooperation with the private sector. It observed, too, that Army training can be useful preparation for skilled personnel and urged that training programs offered by the Army be better designed to meet the needs of industry.

Israel

Because of immigration from eastern and central Europe, Israel in its prestate period had a substantial supply of technically skilled manpower for its very modest industrial establishment. However, the pattern of immigration has shifted over the years, and many unskilled workers from Asia and Africa have joined the labor force since 1960. With growing industrialization, some acute shortages in such fields as electronics, diamond-cutting and weaving began to develop. As a result, the government, and particularly the Ministry of Trade and Industry, has been concerning itself with training for industry, particularly through encouraging expansion of vocational schools, in-plant training, and managerial and professional training at the secondary and university levels.

The Ministry, which has made forecasts of manpower requirements for industry, projected a five-point program as follows: (1) the addition and expansion of two-, three-, and four-year vocational schools for youths to attend both before and during Army service; (2) the opening of additional adult vocational courses; (3) the provision of additional in-plant training; (4) stepped-up promotion and training programs for workers, which are to be run by industry or the government; (5) encouragement of immigration of skilled workers from abroad. The Ministry also estimates in 1970 only about one-half of industry's needs for managers, scientists, and engineers are being met from existing university resources and that there will have to be a substantial expansion of higher education.

Notes

1. Adapted from Republic of the Philippines, Department of Commerce and Industry, Technical Staff, *Guidelines for Foreign Investors in the Philippines* (Manila: Department of Commerce and Industry, n.d.), p. 6.

2. Malaysia, Ministry of Commerce and Industry, Industrial Development Division, *Facilities for Industrial Development* (Kuala Lumpur, 1964), pp. 1-2.

3. Indian Investment Center, *Investing in India. . .Basic Facts of the Indian Economy* (New Delhi, 1962), Foreword.

4. *Ibid.*, p. 35.

5. A full account of the Indian experience with programs to aid small industries is found in India, Ministry of Industry, *Report of the International Perspective Planning Teams* (New Delhi, 1963).

6. Indian Investment Center, *op. cit.*

7. Iran, *Outline of the Third Plan* 1341-1346 [September 1962-March 1968](Teheran: Plan Organization, 1342 [1963]).

8. Israel, Ministry of Trade and Industry, Planning Division, *Programme for Israel's Industrial Development, Second Outline, 1965-1970*, trans. Hannah Schmorak (Jerusalem: Hatchiya Printing Press, Ltd.), Foreword.

9. *Ibid.*, p. 42.

10. Recommended in Mission of the International Bank for Reconstruction and Development, *Report on the Economic Aspects of Malaysia* (Baltimore: Johns Hopkins Press, July 1963).

11. Malaysia, Ministry of Commerce and Industry, Industrial Development Division, *Notes for the Guidance of Applicants for Tariff Concessions* (Kuala Lumpur, October 1961).

12. Indian Investment Center, *op. cit.*

13. John P. Lewis, *Quiet Crisis in India* (Washington: the Brookings Institution, 1962), pp. 228-29.

14. Israel, Ministry of Trade and Industry, *op. cit.*, p. 195.

15. The International Bank for Reconstruction and Development, *Economic Development of Malaya*, Report of a Mission organized by the IBRD at the request of the government of the Federation of Malaya, the Crown Colony of Singapore, and the United Kingdom (Baltimore: Johns Hopkins Press, 1955).

16. Lewis, *op. cit.*

17. Pakistan, *The Second Five-Year Plan, 1960-1965, Including Revised Estimates* (Karachi: Planning Commission, 1961).

18. Iran, *op. cit.*

7   **Conclusions**

The concern of governments in modernizing societies with accumulating capital for development purposes has led to the expansion of institutions able to attract the savings of individual citizens. It has also caused governments to make use of public and quasi-public savings funds, such as the Malaysian Employees' Provident Fund and various other insurance funds.

The allocation of resources for development purposes occurs most frequently through development banks and corporations, capitalized usually through direct governmental appropriations and international loans or grants. Sometimes these institutions acquire capital through public subscription, which may serve as another means of drawing on private savings. Development corporations may have a special purpose (e.g., the encouragement of small industries or of a particular industry, such as tourism), or may operate within sublimits of the political structure, as in the case of India's state financial corporations. Sometimes international organizations such as the Commonwealth Development Fund and the World Bank are important agents for capital dissemination for development.

The provision of advice and inducements to the private sector, particularly to encourage industrialization, is extensive and varied. Advisory services, such as feasibility studies, market analyses, technical advice, guidance in cost and quality control and in marketing and promotion, are all employed. Inducements such as tax holidays, favorable terms for depreciation and plant amortization, and encouragement of research and manpower training, are frequently proffered. The provision of infrastructure such as roads, power, and water, sometimes within the confines of industrial estates, is a growing part of governmental efforts to foster industrialization. Note should also be taken of the use of protective tariffs to encourage new industries and of the multitude of training activities that governments directly or indirectly subsidize in order to provide industry with qualified manpower.

Several general comments relevant to the foregoing survey of experience with private sector participation may be made regarding policies and programs for encouraging the private sector to perform in accordance with national development goals.

The patterns which emerge from an examination of individual countries experiences perhaps reflect more the inherent character and dynamics of the country than they do any clearly identifiable rules for economic development with general applicability. The contrast of India's elaborate system of regulation and control and Israel's reliance on broad governmental guidance and the market reflects differences in philosophical and political approaches, as well as variations in geography and the problems they are seeking to solve.

However, in spite of each country's uniqueness, there are, as was noted in the conclusion to Part 1, certain common needs and characteristics in virtually all modernizing nations. Capital for development is always in short supply; manpower capabilities are usually not congruent with the requirements of industry; entrepreneurship characteristically needs to be stimulated through the provision of special inducements. Thus, good reason exists for the exchange of experience in these areas among the countries engaged in modernization. New approaches may be discovered; pitfalls avoided; and perhaps, in particular, encouragement received to explore a variety of routes to development.

When the limited involvement of the private sector in development planning is considered in connection with the present discussion, it seems clear that most policies and programs to encourage private-sector performance are arrived at with very little advice or assistance from that sector. It can be argued that consultation is unnecessary when benefits are to be offered. However, it is difficult to see how benefits can be made most relevant and economic in the absence of an opportunity for government to hear about the problems, interests, and needs of the private sector.

Implied, then, are arrangements which go beyond the involvement of the private sector at significant stages in the formal governmental planning process—important as that is. For until governments have the counsel of the private sector in the formulation of the policies and programs that implement broad plans, the objectives in many instances may not be achieved. This is not to say that unusual prescience abides in the private sector or that governments should not, as they in fact must, be the final arbiters of public policies. It is simply to say that the practical experience of the private sector, its contact with the realities of the marketplace, its values and motivations, should be available to inform governmental policies and action programs. This may be done in many ways: through consultation at the stage of executive and legislative policy formulation; through the frequent use of advisory committees from industry; through informal consultation and collaboration; and through specific steps to assure that private-sector experience with public policies and inducements is regularly fed back to the government.

Finally, two steps may be suggested. The first of these grows out of the observation that in very few of the modernizing countries is serious, coherent attention given to how the private sector may become more intimately and relevantly involved in the planning process. As a corollary, there are few instances of concerted evaluation of the whole range of actual and potential policies and programs for private-sector stimulation that governments might pursue. To begin to remedy these limitations, some governments may wish to create a prestigious high-level body made up of appropriate government and private-sector officials to assess the entire subject of private-sector involvement in the processes of planning and socioeconomic development. To avoid unduly dispersing its energies, this body might concentrate first on how to involve the private sector more effectively in the public-planning processes. Then it might take up, perhaps through subcommittees and in the course of time, such specific policies and practices as tax benefits for new and expanding industry; manpower-training problems; selected aspects of infrastructure development, etc. As an aid to the perspectives that this body can bring to bear, some of its members could perhaps visit other modernizing countries, to become familiar at first hand with certain of their planning, policy, and procedural experiences.

The second type of action is concerned with the development of closer communication between government, on the one hand,

and important individual industries within a country, on the other. A prototype is to be found in the national conference sponsored by the Organization of American States in Uruguay in 1967. This conference assembled leading government officials from the Ministry of Finance, the Office of Planning, the Ministry of Foreign Affairs, the Ministry of Industry and Commerce, the Ministry of Labor and Social Security, etc., and a number of key individuals from the private sector associated with the woolen textile industry, the principal industry in Uruguay. The focus of the conference was on participation of the private sector in the definition and execution of economic policies and programs, with special reference to the woolen textile industry.

Given the need to delve deeply into the unique circumstances and requirements of individual industries or industry groupings, it seems likely that approaches of this kind are called for in many of the modernizing nations. The sponsors may be intracountry agencies, either official, such as offices of national planning, or private, such as unions of chambers of commerce or national management associations; or they may be international bodies, such as the World Bank, the Inter-American Development Bank, the Organization of American States, or the United Nations, perhaps through its economic commissions for Asia, Africa, and Latin America. Conferences that center on government planning, and associated policies and programs for encouraging private performance to assist in plan fulfillment, when built around the needs and interests of individual industries, offer one hopeful route toward the establishment of relationships between the public and the private sectors. If the results of such efforts are made available to the high-level body proposed above, informed decisions may emerge that go far toward the goal of involving the private sector in realistic and productive ways in the processes of government planning and implementation.

About the Author

John C. Honey is Vice-President for Government Affairs and Research at Syracuse University. A professor of government and public administration, he has been Associate Director of the Institute of Public Administration and a consultant to the Ford Foundation, the Department of State, NASA, and other federal agencies. He has contributed numerous articles on science and government, program planning and programming techniques, and organization to the *Public Administration Review*, the *Annals* of the American Academy of Political and Social Science, the *Federal Bar Journal*, the *Saturday Review*, and other journals and is the author of *Higher Education for Public Service* and *Toward Strategies for Public Administration Development in Latin America* and the coauthor of *Administration of Large-Scale Research Organizations* and *Attitudes of Scientists and Engineers About Government Employment.* In addition, Dr. Honey has served as a supervisory editor of National Science Foundation publications and as a member of the editorial board of the *Public Administration Review* and a Trustee of the Inter-University Public Administration Case Program. He is a graduate of Columbia University (Bard College), and holds a Ph.D. in public service from Syracuse.